BRAIN GAMES™ kids

pil

Publications International, Ltd

Puzzle Constructors: Mark Danna, Helene Hovanec, Allison Lassieur, Vicky Shiotsu

Illustrators: Bryan Babiarz, Giuseppe Conserti, Lisa Covington, Alysen Hiller, Sari Rantanen, Dave Roberts, Marilyn Roberts

Louis Weber, CEO
Publications International, Ltd.
7373 North Cicero Avenue
Lincolnwood, Illinois 60712

ISBN-13: 978-1-60553-156-4
ISBN-10: 1-60553-156-1

Manufactured in China.

8 7 6 5 4 3 2 1

CONTENTS

IT'S ALL FUN AND GAMES!

Hey Kids! Are you ready to have some fun?

Here's the easiest question in *Brain Games™: Kids:* What's the best way to get the most out of this big book of puzzles? The answer: Read this page first!

We've assembled a huge collection of fun puzzles for you to tackle. You'll find mazes, crosswords, word puzzles, math puzzles—you name it, we've got it! Try to work a variety of different puzzles each time you open this book. That's the best way to give your brain the biggest boost. Other things to keep in mind:

• The puzzles have been sorted into levels, which means you'll find the easiest puzzles at the beginning of the book. If you're really looking for a challenge, head straight to Level 5. Those puzzles are the hardest!

• You can find answers to every puzzle at the back of the book. Just be sure to give each puzzle a fair try before peeking at the answers. You want to be sure to give your brain a full workout before calling for help.

• No matter what puzzle you're working on—whether you solve it in a snap or get hung up on it for what seems like ages—the most important thing to remember is to have fun!

Now you're ready to get started! Every day is a great day for puzzles, so don't wait for a rainy day. (It will just get the pages wet anyway!)

Hello Parents—

The pages of *Brain Games™: Kids* are jammed with an exciting collection of crossword puzzles, word games, mazes, and much more. These puzzles will help your kids give their brains a boost—and the kids will have lots of fun working them! They'll improve their language skills, logical thinking, and analytic reasoning without even realizing it.

We've grouped the puzzles by difficulty level so that you can help guide your child to the puzzles that will suit him or her best. Beginners will love working on the puzzles in Level 1—these easy puzzles are a great way for kids to get a feel for *Brain Games™*. Intermediates will eat up the food for thought in the middle sections (Levels 2 and 3), while advanced puzzlers will love the challenge of the mental marathon of puzzles in Levels 4 and 5. The answers are included at the end of the book, so if they get stuck (or if you do!), just take a peek at the solution to get back on track.

Many educators agree that puzzles and games are among the best ways to engage children in the thinking process. Your mission is to get them started on the journey toward learning. So give them this book and turn them loose on puzzling!

Letter T Match

Draw a line from each **T** word to its matching picture.

Tepee

Tree

Truck

Tiger

Triangle

Tricycle

Answers on page 177.

Word Play

Place 1 letter in each blank space to spell a word that means the opposite of the word on the left. Then read down to answer this riddle: What is the happiest state?

Divide	___ U L T I P L Y
Below	___ B O V E
Smooth	___ O U G H
Old	___ O U N G
Tighten	___ O O S E N
Present	___ B S E N T
Wide	___ A R R O W
Easy	___ I F F I C U L T

Answer: _____

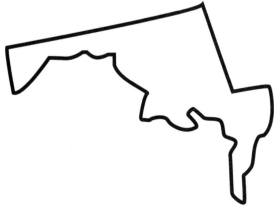

Answers on page 177.

7

Choose Wisely!

Circle the word that best finishes the sentence. Read carefully!

1. Mr. Weber works (hard, hand).

2. Frank drives a (card, car).

3. Maria likes (dolls, dulls, dills).

4. Leroy drinks (mild, milk, mill).

5. Leah picks (roses, rises).

6. Judd eats (meat, mate, meant).

7. Debbie plays the (flute, float).

8. Jill and Julie are best (pals, pails, pills).

9. Watch out! There's a hive filled with (beans, bears, bees).

10. Holli runs (fast, frost, fact).

Answers on page 177.

What Not to Wear?

Circle the item of clothing that doesn't belong with the others in each group.

Answers on page 177.

A Fruity Puzzle

The words below name different kinds of fruit. Each letter is missing a stroke. Add the missing lines to see the names of the fruits. If you need help, look at the pictures.

1.  HFFI C

2.  I CMNA

3.  NKHNGF

4.  LRKHFCS

5.  FCHLFCS

6.  CLFFKV

7.  STKHVBFKKV

8.  VHTFFMCI MN

Answers on page 177.

What's Your Number?

Write each number word in the grid. We put a few letters in place to get you started.

3 Letters

One

Six

Ten

Two

4 Letters

Five

Four

Nine

5 Letters

Eight

Seven

Three

Answers on page 177.

11

What's at the Theater?

There's a letter missing from each word below. Each word refers to something at a theater. Use one of the 5 letters we've given you. After you've used one, you can cross it off because each letter will be used only once.

S E A V C

1. M O __ I E

2. P O P __ O R N

3. __ O D A

4. T I C K __ T S

5. C __ N D Y

Answers on page 177.

Number Crossword

Use the clues to help fill in the puzzle with number words.

ACROSS

1. Number of items sold in a pair
2. Number of seasons in a year
3. Number of arms on an octopus
6. Number of fingers on 2 hands
9. Number of years in a century
10. Number of days in a week
11. Number of minutes in an hour

DOWN

1. Number of months that begin with the letter **J**
2. Number of sides on a pentagon
4. Number of nickels in a dollar

5. Number of items in a dozen
7. Number of players on a baseball field
8. Number of wheels on a unicycle
10. Number of legs on an insect

Answers on page 177.

A Different Order

Sometimes the letters of a word can be placed in a different order to spell a new word. These are called **anagrams.** Draw a line from each word on the left to its anagram on the right.

Mope	Tar
Peas	Bare
Free	Live
Bear	Poem
Coin	Reef
Scat	Aunt
Tuna	Last
Evil	Apes
Rate	Ion
Salt	Cats

Answers on page 177.

14

Frame-Up

Fill in the puzzle frame with words that match the clues below. Each word shares 1 or 2 letters with the word that comes after it. Start each word in the same space as its clue number. When you get to a corner, follow the direction of the arrow.

Clues

1. You can borrow reading materials from your local _____.

2. There are 365 days in one _____.

3. A painter or sculptor is an _____.

4. The red octagonal sign on the road tells drivers to _____.

5. You write in ink with a _____.

6. The opposite of always is _____.

7. If you make a writing mistake in pencil, you can _____ it.

8. The opposite of buy is _____.

9. A scientist works in a _____.

10. You can spread cream cheese on a toasted _____.

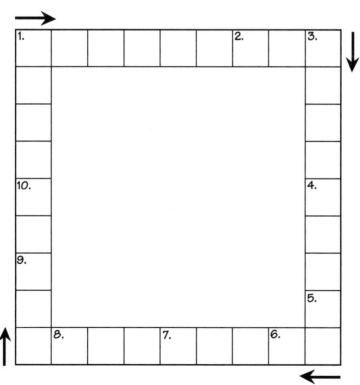

Answers on page 177.

Pen It In

Use the clues to add letters to the word **PEN** to make new words.

1. Opposite of shut: ____ P E N

2. What you do with money: ____ P E N ____

3. Used to write with: P E N ____ ____ ____

4. Not a dime or a nickel: P E N ____ ____

5. A bird that can't fly: P E N ____ ____ ____ ____

Answers on page 177.

Works of Art

Use the letters of the word **ART** to complete each word below.

1.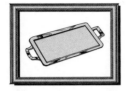
   | | | | Y |

2.
   | S | | | |

3.
   | | | | | I | N |

4.
   | H | E | | | |

5.
   | E | | | | H |

6.
   | F | E | | | H | E | |

7.
   | | | | I | | N | G | L | E |

Answers on page 177.

Flower Fun

Can you find these 16 items hidden in the picture?

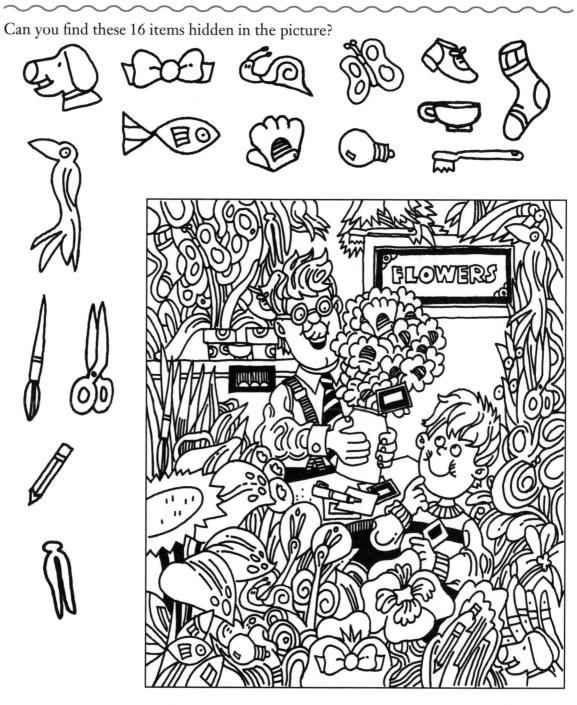

Answers on page 178.

Middle Management

Fill in the blanks in the center row by making 3-letter words in each column. If you fill in the correct letters, the middle row will spell out a word, too. **Hint:** In some cases, you can make more than one 3-letter word by choosing a different middle letter. So choose wisely!

A   J   A   O   O   F   I   W

☐ ☐ ☐ ☐ ☐ ☐ ☐ ☐

K   M   Y   D   N   X   Y   Y

Answer: _____

Answers on page 178.

Picture Crossword

Look at the pictures on this page, and name each one. Then write the word in the correct numbered spaces. Be sure to check to see if the word should be written across or down.

ACROSS

1.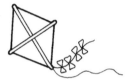

3.

5.

6.

DOWN

1.

2.

4.

Answers on page 178.

State Lines

Put each state name into the grid in alphabetical order. Then read down the starred column to find the name of another state. Cross off each word after you write it into the grid.

UTAH

OHIO

KENTUCKY

MISSOURI

ALASKA

OKLAHOMA

PENNSYLVANIA

COLORADO

MAINE

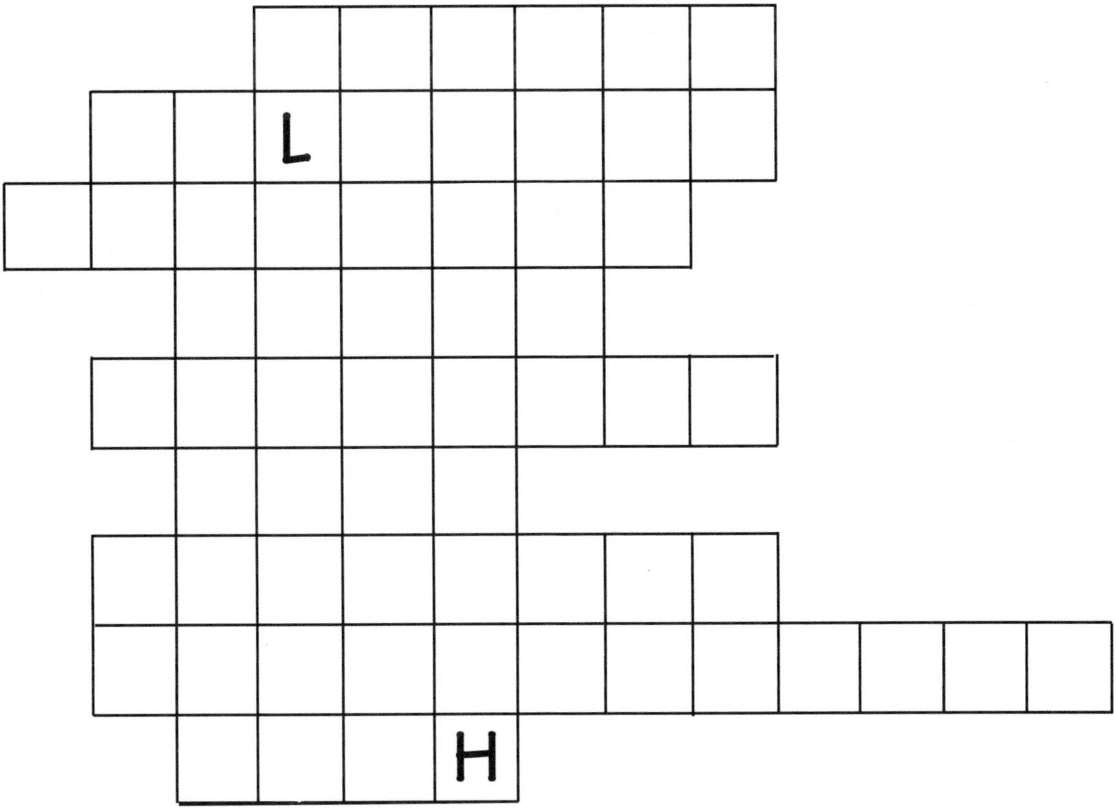

Answers on page 178.

21

Rhyme Time

It's time to rhyme! Draw a line connecting the objects that rhyme. The first one has been done for you.

Answers on page 178.

Sweet Spot

Some people like to sleep with sugar under their pillows. Want to know why? To solve this riddle, copy the letters from the list into the numbered spaces below. We've placed the letter **A** for you.

A 8, 11, 22   **O** 2

C 7   **R** 20

D 19   **S** 1, 14, 24

E 5, 13, 16, 17, 21   **T** 3, 18

H 4, 10   **V** 12

M 23   **W** 15

N 9   **Y** 6

$$\frac{}{1}\ \frac{}{2}\qquad\frac{}{3}\ \frac{}{4}\ \frac{}{5}\ \frac{}{6}\qquad\frac{}{7}\ \frac{A}{8}\ \frac{}{9}$$

$$\frac{}{10}\ \frac{A}{11}\ \frac{}{12}\ \frac{}{13}\qquad\frac{}{14}\ \frac{}{15}\ \frac{}{16}\ \frac{}{17}\ \frac{}{18}$$

$$\frac{}{19}\ \frac{}{20}\ \frac{}{21}\ \frac{A}{22}\ \frac{}{23}\ \frac{}{24}\,!$$

Answer on page 178.

Jungle Maze

Professor Stanley is trying to find a safe path to the nest of the Klum-Klum bird. Can you help him?

Answer on page 178.

24

Sheepish Riddle

Name each picture below, and write the word in the spaces. Then copy each boxed letter to the correct numbered blank at the bottom of the page. Read the letters to find the answer to this riddle: Where do sheep get their hair cut?

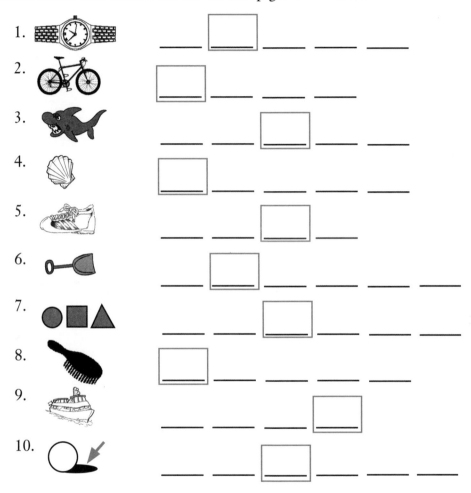

Answer:

At the ___ ___ ___   ___ ___ ___   ___ ___ ___ ___
        8   1   3   2   7   10   4   6   5   9

Answers on page 178.

C-Ya

The **C** sound can be soft like an **S** or hard like a **K**. Fill in the blanks to these words with either a **C, S,** or **K.** The pictures are clues to what the words are.

1. F A _____ E

2. _____ U N

3. _____ O R N

4. B O O _____

5. _____ H U R _____ H

6. _____ L O _____ _____

7. _____ H I _____ _____ E N

Answers on page 178.

Line Trace

Here's a picture that was made with 1 long line. The artist never picked up his pen when drawing it. Follow the line with your finger. Can you find the end of it? Start where the arrow points.

In Outer Space

Help the alien find the hidden words. Start with **S**, and then go around the path clockwise. Write down every third letter (the first third letter is **U**) until you have written 8 words related to outer space.

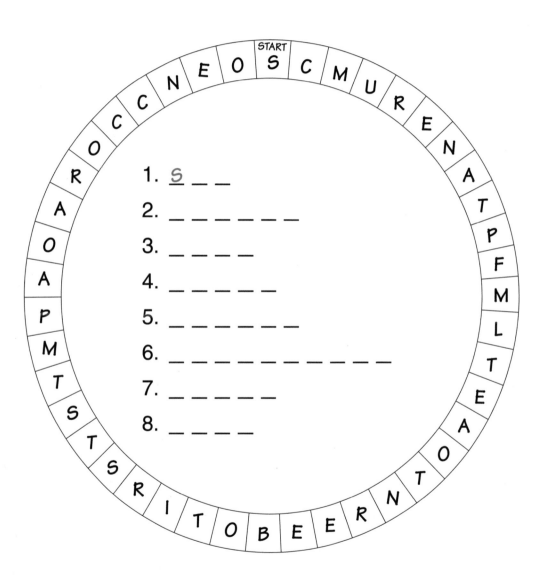

START

1. S _ _
2. _ _ _ _ _ _
3. _ _ _ _
4. _ _ _ _ _
5. _ _ _ _ _ _
6. _ _ _ _ _ _ _ _ _
7. _ _ _ _ _
8. _ _ _ _

Answers on page 178.

Tiny Creatures

Write one of the 6 letters in an empty space to complete the name of each tiny creature you might see in the park. Cross off each letter as you use it.

B M A W S F

1. ___ N T

2. ___ E E

3. ___ L Y

4. ___ O T H

5. ___ N A I L

6. ___ A S P

Gigantic Creatures

Write one of the 6 letters in an empty space to complete the name of each gigantic creature you might see in the zoo. Cross off each letter as you use it.

G H E P R C

1. ___ Y T H O N

2. ___ R O C O D I L E

3. ___ I P P O P O T A M U S

4. ___ H I N O C E R O S

5. ___ I R A F F E

6. ___ L E P H A N T

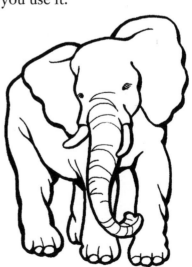

Answers on page 179.

'Tis the Season

The answers to the clues are words related to seasons or weather. Fill in the blanks, and then write the circled letters on the numbered lines to answer this riddle: What is a frog's favorite time of year?

1. The season after fall __ O __ __ __ __

2. A small shallow pool of water left after the rain O __ __ __ __ __ __

3. Soft flakes of ice O __ __ __

4. A flash of light in the sky __ __ __ __ O __ __ __ __

5. A cloud that is close to the earth's surface __ __ O

6. A strong wind with rain __ __ __ O __

7. The season after spring __ __ __ __ O __

8. Moving air __ O __ __

9. A loud rumbling or cracking sound __ __ __ O __ __ __

10. Another name for "fall" __ __ __ __ O __

Answer:

__ __ __ __ __ __ __ __ __ __ !
3   2   6   8   9   5   4   1   10   7

Answers on page 179.

30

Picture Word Search

The names of the 7 items pictured below are hidden in the grid. Words may run forward or backward, up or down, or diagonally, but they are always in a straight line.

P	Z	I	X	H	S	X	L
M	S	K	H	C	T	F	R
O	B	H	P	N	B	K	H
H	O	J	I	A	R	M	E
Y	A	H	G	R	Y	P	A
E	R	H	D	B	T	P	R
X	W	X	D	O	C	A	T
D	O	O	R	I	J	L	W

Answers on page 179.

What Am I?

This is a countdown of 10 statements about a thing. How many clues will it take for you to figure out what it is?

10. I'm seen on city streets.

9. I'm often made up of lots of people.

8. I'm often filled with loud music.

7. I often show up on holidays and for celebrations.

6. People in me usually move in groups.

5. Around New Year's Day in Pasadena, California, I include wonderful designs made of roses.

4. On Thanksgiving Day in New York City, I have big balloons.

3. I often have marching bands and baton twirlers.

2. People stand along curbs to watch me pass by.

1. I am an event.

What am I?

Answer on page 179.

M Is for Many States

Name all 8 U.S. states that begin with the letter **M.** Then list the states in alphabetical order.

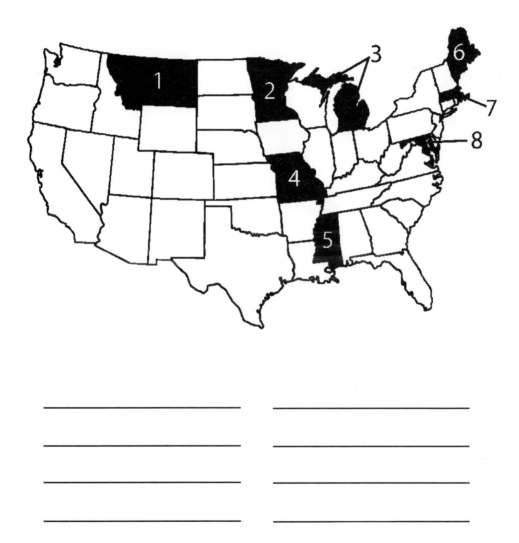

_____   _____

_____   _____

_____   _____

_____   _____

Answers on page 179.

Star Search

Read the letters below, and move them to the blanks. Do all letters in order under the ringed planets first, then the stars, and finally the moons. When you're done, you'll see that our prediction came true!

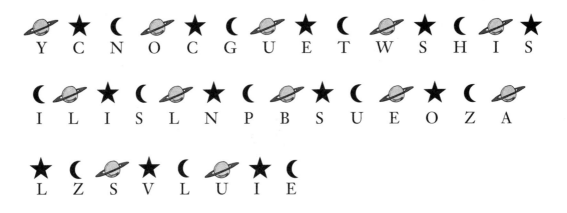

Y C N O C G U E T W S H I S

I L I S L N P B S U E O Z A

L Z S V L U I E

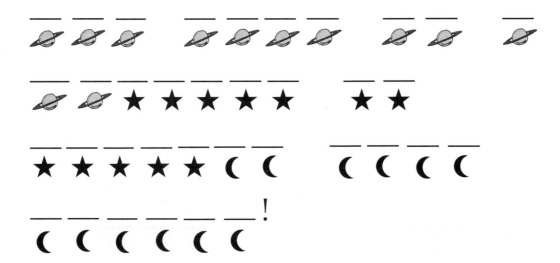

Answer on page 179.

Picture Crossword

Look at the pictures on this page, and name each one. Then write the word in the correct numbered spaces. Be sure to check to see if the word should be written across or down.

ACROSS

1.

3.

5.

6.

7.

DOWN

1.

2.

3.

4.

Answers on page 179.

Wild Cats

Place each wild cat into the grid. There are some letters already in place to get you running.

4 Letters
Lion

5 Letters
Tiger

6 Letters
Cougar

Jaguar

7 Letters
Cheetah

Leopard

Panther

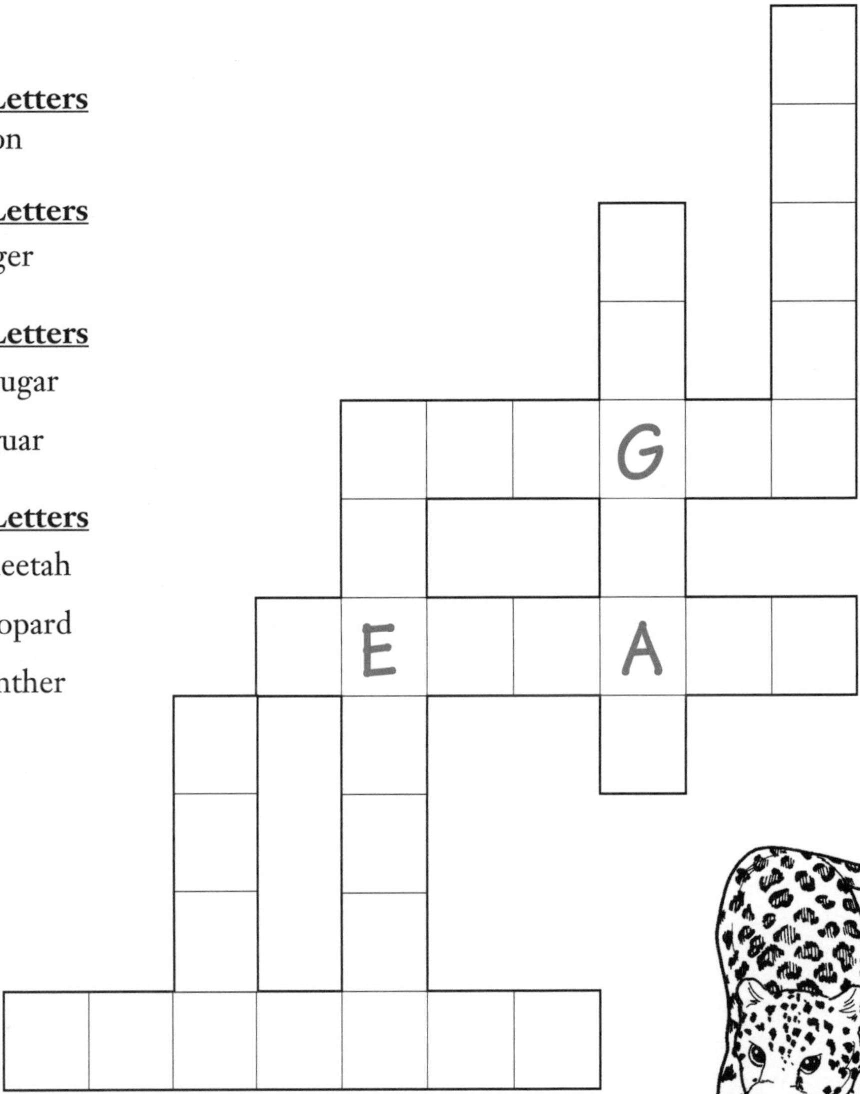

Answers on page 179.

Cross It Out

Follow the cross-out instructions for the letters in the grid. Then, take the leftover letters and put them in the blank spaces below. Go from left to right and top to bottom, and you will answer this riddle: What goes up but never comes down?

Cross out 3 **B**'s

Cross out 4 **C**'s

Cross out 2 **D**'s

Cross out 4 **F**'s

Cross out 3 **H**'s

Cross out 2 **I**'s

Cross out 3 **J**'s

Cross out 2 **K**'s

Cross out 3 **L**'s

Cross out 4 **M**'s

Cross out 3 **N**'s

Cross out 3 **P**'s

Cross out 2 **Q**'s

Cross out 4 **S**'s

B	Y	J	F	F	F	F
I	B	J	I	N	N	O
U	P	B	S	S	N	J
Q	P	S	S	R	L	H
Q	P	K	A	L	C	H
D	M	K	L	C	G	C
D	M	E	M	M	C	H

Answer: ___ ___ ___ ___   ___ ___ __

Answer on page 179.

Weather or Not

Name each picture below, and write the word on the line next to it. Then copy the first letter of each word on the correct numbered blank at the bottom of the page. Read the letters to find the name of something you might need in snowy weather.

1.
   _____

2.
   _____

3.
   _____

4.
   _____

5.
   _____

6.
   _____

Answer: ___ ___ ___ ___ ___ ___
         1   2   3   4   5   6

Answer on page 179.

Front and Back

Fill in the puzzle frame with words that match the clues below. Each word shares 1 or 2 letters with the word that comes after it. Start each word in the same space as its clue number. When you get to a corner, follow the direction of the arrow.

Clues

1. A mistake

2. Opposite of smooth

3. An African doglike mammal

4. The nut from the oak tree

5. Drums and horns can be this

6. To move over or make way

7. Miniature

8. A long, silver musical instrument

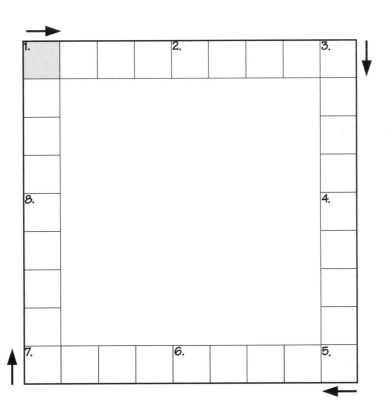

Answers on page 179.

TURN THE HEAT UP

Charlie's Painting

Read the clues to find out which picture Charlie painted. As you read each clue, cross out the picture it describes. The picture that is left is the one that Charlie painted.

Clues

1. It does not begin with **D.**

2. It does not end with **L.**

3. It does not begin with **H.**

4. It does not begin with **S.**

5. It does not end with **P.**

6. It does not end with **B.**

7. It does not begin with **F.**

8. It does not end with **G.**

Answer on page 179.

Beginnings and Endings

Each of the words below begins and ends with the same letter. Use the clues to figure out each word.

1. ___ ___ ___   Another word for mother

2. ___ ___ ___ ___   Sound a lion makes

3. ___ ___ ___ ___ ___ ___   A kind of "weepy" tree

4. ___ ___ ___ ___ ___   Rap one's knuckles on a door

5. ___ ___ ___ ___ ___ ___ ___   Opposite of failure

6. ___ ___ ___ ___   Sound a chick makes

7. ___ ___ ___ ___ ___   To remove a pencil mark

8. ___ ___ ___ ___ ___ ___ ___   Male chicken

9. ___ ___ ___ ___ ___ ___   Curtains often hang over this

10. ___ ___ ___ ___   To strike with a foot

11. ___ ___ ___ ___   Person, place, or thing

Answers on page 180.

Dyeing to Be Found

One color is hidden between 2 or more words in each silly sentence below. Underline each color as you find it (ignore any punctuation between words). Here are 6 of the colors you'll be looking for:

AQUA, HAZEL, PEACH, PUMPKIN, ROSE, and RUBY.

You'll have to find the other colors without any hints. We did the first for you.

1. <u>Can a rye</u> bread be used for sandwiches?

2. Has the haze lifted yet?

3. Did you stop in Ken's house?

4. They work in a quarry.

5. Here's the grub you like.

6. If you hit her, she'll yell "Ow!"

7. In Jaipur, plenty of people own gems.

8. Is that utensil very old?

9. She won't type a chain letter.

10. The new intro seems fine.

11. Does the ogre enjoy scaring people?

12. The taxicab lacks heat.

13. The water pump kind of fell apart.

14. Where did you go?

15. You can now hit each golf ball.

Answers on page 180.

Don't Miss the Bus (Part 1)

There won't be a quiz at school today, but there will be one on the school bus. First, study this picture for 2 minutes. Then turn the page and answer the 10 questions. Seven or more correct answers puts you in the driver's seat.

Don't Miss the Bus (Part II)

1. How many kids are standing?

2. What shape are the earrings that the bus driver is wearing?

3. The girl with the braids is sitting in what row from the front?

4. What can be seen on the front lawn of the house in the side window?

5. What are the initials on the cap of the person wearing sunglasses?

6. Where are the hands of the kid who is blowing a bubble?

7. Who can be seen through the back window of the bus?

8. What is the name of the book sticking out of the standing boy's backpack?

9. What is in the right hand of the kid holding the lunch box?

10. The kid with his feet in the air has how many shoes on?

Answers on page 180.

Dollars and Cents

Draw a line from the circle next to each amount on the left to the circle next to its matching amount on the right. Write the letters in order on the matching numbered lines to solve this riddle: What's the difference between an old penny and a new nickel?

2 quarters	1	U	1 dime
3 dimes	2	R	1 dollar bill
2 nickels	3	F	1 half dollar
4 quarters	4	O	1 quarter, 1 nickel
8 nickels	5	C	4 dimes
3 quarters	6	S	8 quarters
7 nickels	7	N	35 pennies
5 quarters	8	E	7 dimes, 1 nickel
2 dollar bills	9	T	125 pennies

Answer: ____ ____ ____ ____ ____ ____ ____ ____ ____
         1   2   3   4   5   6   7   8   9

Answers on page 180.

Filling Good

Complete the word search below to find out which animal's name contains 2 sandwich ingredients. Every word in the word list below is contained within this group of letters. Words can be found horizontally, vertically, or diagonally. They may read backward or forward. Once you find all the words, you can read the hidden message from the remaining letters, left to right, top to bottom.

Word List

Bacon

Bologna

Cheese

Chicken

Egg salad

Lamb

Lettuce

Mayo

Mustard

Onion

Pastrami

Peanut butter

Roast beef

Salami

Spam

Tomato

Tuna fish

Turkey

```
        M  U  S  T  A  R  D
     P  A  S  T  R  A  M  I  E
  T  E  Y  T  B  O  L  O  G  N  A
  H  A  O  E  O  A  N  G  O  Y  L
  T  N  S  S  L  M  S  C  W  E  E
     U  N  A  R  A  A  I  T  K
     T  N  E  L  B  M  T  N  R
     B  S  A  K  A  U  B  O  U
     U  D  J  F  C  M  E  I  T
     T  L  L  E  I  I  I  N  Y
     T  F  M  A  P  S  H  O  I
     E  S  E  S  E  E  H  C  H
     R  O  A  S  T  B  E  E  F
```

Hidden message: _____

Answers on page 180.

Doing Their Jobs

Match the people in Column 1 with the equipment that they need to do their job in Column 2.

Column 1	Column 2
Barber	helmet
Librarian	letters
Dog walker	bag of toys
Football player	map
Janitor	mop
Dentist	whistle
Photographer	pots and pans
Mail carrier	scissors
Cook	toothbrush
Basketball referee	leash
Weatherperson	books
Santa Claus	camera

Answers on page 180.

Forward and Back

Starting at the shaded square, use the clues below to fill in the squares in the grid. The last letter of each word will be the first letter of the next word. Work the puzzle clockwise.

Clues

1. A small bucket
2. King of the jungle
3. Hard material at the end of each finger
4. Opposite of early
5. Opposite of difficult
6. 365 days make one of these
7. A cars drives on this
8. To let something fall to the ground

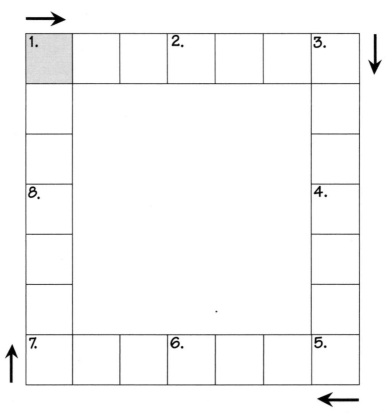

Answers on page 180.

Magic Letters

You don't need a magic wand to change an object into another! Make new words by changing just 1 letter in the name of each of these objects.

1. Change a  into a

_____   _____

2. Change a into a

_____   _____

3. Change a into a

_____   _____

4. Change into

_____   _____

5. Change a into a

_____   _____

Answers on page 180.

Picture This

You'll find an "instant" picture hiding inside this puzzle. To see the picture, color in each puzzle piece that has 2 dots.

Answer on page 181.

Fly Away Home

Unscramble this sentence by writing the letter in the alphabet that comes after each of these letters (Z=A, A=B, B=C, etc.). When you're done, you'll reveal a fun fact about some of your favorite flying creatures!

___ ___ ___   ___ ___ ___ ___ ___ ___ ___
S G D   L N M Z Q B G

___ ___ ___ ___ ___ ___ ___ ___ ___   ___ ___ ___ ___ ___ ___ ___ ___
A T S S D Q E K X   L H F Q Z S D R

___ ___ ___ ___ ___   ___ ___ ___
R N T S G   E N Q

___ ___ ___   ___ ___ ___ ___ ___ ___,   ___ ___ ___ ___
S G D   V H M S D Q   I T R S

___ ___   ___ ___ ___ ___
Z R   L Z M X

___ ___ ___ ___ ___   ___ ___.
A H Q C R   C N

Answer on page 181.

Let It BE

Each of the words in this puzzle begins with the letters **B** and **E**. Can you BEnd your brain around all 10? The clues in parentheses will help.

1. B E ____ (insect that makes honey)

2. B E ____ ____ (it rings at church)

3. B E ____ ____ (better than better)

4. B E ____ ____ ____ (fruit starting with blue or straw)

5. B E ____ ____ ____ ____ (mind your manners)

6. B E ____ ____ ____ ____ ____ (place to sleep)

7. B E ____ ____ ____ ____ ____ ____ ____ (the start of a story)

8. B E ____ ____ ____ ____ ____ (short reply to "Why can't I?")

9. B E ____ ____ ____ ____ ____ ____ ____ (prettier than pretty)

Answers on page 181.

Picture Crossword

Look at the pictures on this page, and name each one. Then write the word in the correct numbered spaces. Be sure to check to see if the word should be written across or down.

ACROSS

1.

3.

5.

6.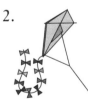

7.

DOWN

1.

2.

3.

4.

Answers on page 181.

Round Up

Eight words are hidden in these circles. To find the hidden words, start at one of the letters and read either clockwise or counterclockwise. All the words have something in common.

1.
```
  e b
l      e
  t e
```
_____

2.
```
  c k
i      e
  r c t
```
_____

3.
```
  r n
o      e
  h t
```
_____

4.
```
  o c
c      h
k      c
  r o a
```
_____

5.
```
  u b y
t        l
  t e r f
```
_____

6.
```
  u q s
i        o
          m
  t o
```
_____

7.
```
  h s s
o        a
          r
p        g
  p e r
```
_____

8.
```
  a g o n
r          f
d y l
```
_____

Answers on page 181.

Subtract or Add

Find all the math problems with the correct answer of 10, and write the letter on the blanks below. Read from left to right, top to bottom. Then you'll find the answer to this riddle: What do you call a ship that lies on the bottom of the ocean and shakes?

10+0 A	9+2 K	11−1 N	5+5 E	4+3 O	8+4 K
9+1 R	13+5 H	5+6 I	8+2 V	13−3 O	4+6 U
7+4 C	12+1 X	3+7 S	10+0 W	14+3 O	14−4 R
13−3 E	9+0 B	1+9 C	0+10 K		

Answer: ___ ___ ___ ___ ___ ___ ___ ___ ___ ___ ___ ___!

Answer on page 181.

Synonym Unscramble

Synonyms are words that mean the same thing. For example, **HAPPY** means the same thing as **GLAD.** Unscramble the synonym for each of the following words. Use the clues in the parentheses to help you.

1. TUPSE (sad) _____

2. LERCU (mean) _____

3. LECKUCH (laugh) _____

4. FABUITLEU (very pretty) _____

5. HOPTO (picture) _____

6. PRIT (vacation) _____

7. GREENTSTINI (fascinating) _____

8. TORPS (game) _____

9. RASCY (frightening) _____

10. ITSSECAU (luggage) _____

11. CODROT (physician) _____

12. AWRD (sketch) _____

Answers on page 181.

Egg-cellent!

Hidden in the picture are a bunch of Easter eggs. Hop to it, and find as many as you can. Finding 20 or more would be *egg*-citing!

Answers on page 181.

Weather Compounds

Use the code in the box to help you answer each question with a compound word.

A	B	C	D	E	F	G	H	I	J	K	L	M
1	2	3	4	5	6	7	8	9	10	11	12	13
N	O	P	Q	R	S	T	U	V	W	X	Y	Z
14	15	16	17	18	19	20	21	22	23	24	25	26

1. What is often seen in the sky after a shower?

___ ___ ___ ___ ___ ___ ___
18   1   9   14   2   15   23

2. What beams in the sky each morning?

___ ___ ___ ___ ___ ___ ___ ___
19   21   14   12   9   7   8   20

3. What small, thin, frozen particles fall from the sky in winter?

___ ___ ___ ___ ___ ___ ___ ___ ___ ___
19   14   15   23   6   12   1   11   5   19

4. What do you call a sudden, heavy rainfall?

___ ___ ___ ___ ___ ___ ___ ___ ___ ___
3   12   15   21   4   2   21   18   19   20

5. What is a small breeze that moves in circles?

___ ___ ___ ___ ___ ___ ___ ___ ___
23   8   9   18   12   23   9   14   4

6. What is a round piece of ice that falls like rain?

___ ___ ___ ___ ___ ___ ___ ___ ___
8   1   9   12   19   20   15   14   5

Answers on page 181.

Tricky Triangles

How many triangles are in each picture below? Be careful! Some triangles might be hidden.

1.

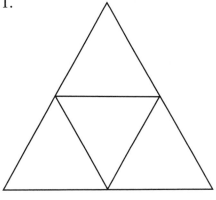

_____ triangles

2.

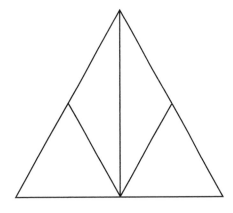

_____ triangles

3.

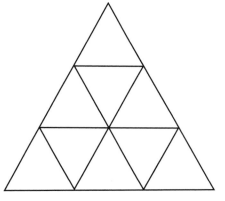

_____ triangles

4.

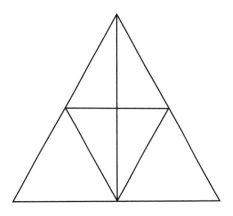

_____ triangles

Answers on page 181.

Triplets

Some letters in the grid below appear 3 times. Cross those letters out. Put the leftover letters into the spaces below. Go from left to right and top to bottom to answer this riddle: What pets don't mind getting stepped on?

1.

Z	Z	I	I	D	D	D	Y
Z	I	C	L	L	L	Y	Y
O	V	V	N	U	U	U	A
V	O	Q	N	R	J	J	G
Q	K	O	N	M	J	P	G
H	K	Q	K	M	M	G	F
E	H	H	W	W	T	F	F
B	B	B	S	W	X	X	X

Answer: __ __ __ __ __ __ __

Now, do the same thing here to answer this riddle: What rooms cannot be entered?

2.

M	K	G	T	T	I
B	V	Q	T	E	U
B	Q	V	K	S	E
K	H	B	V	P	E
Q	W	J	G	R	P
F	P	O	N	I	D
W	J	C	N	D	A
W	C	G	I	D	O
C	N	F	M	L	A
L	S	J	L	F	A

Answer: __ __ __ __ __ __ __ __ __

Answers on page 181.

Cool Codes

The answer to the following saying is in code. Each picture stands for 1 letter. Write the correct letter above each picture to figure out the saying.

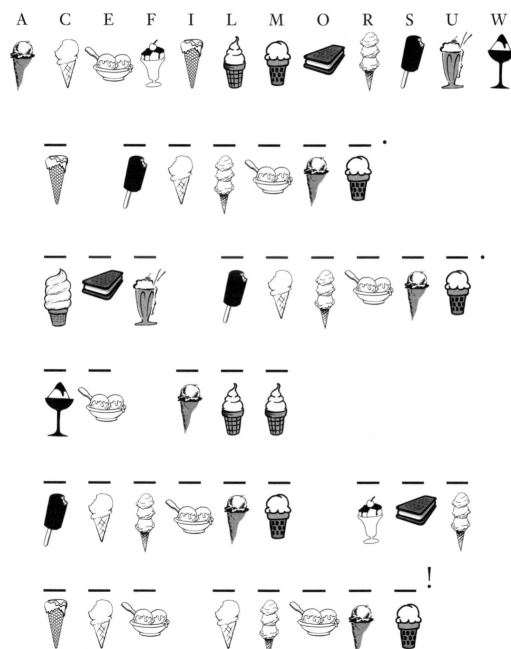

Answer on page 181.

Animal Actions

Complete the puzzle with words from the box below.

leap	perch	climb	swing	gallop	slither
peck	soar	nibble	plunge	burrow	crawl

ACROSS

1. Sway

3. Scale a mountain

4. Dive

7. Creep

8. Jump

10. Sit

11. Fly

DOWN

2. Chew

4. Tap with beak

5. Run

6. Slide

9. Dig

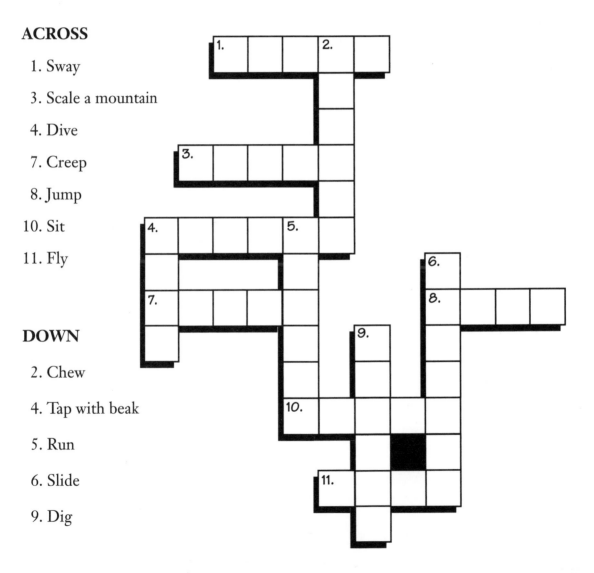

Answers on page 181.

Farmer Pete's Riddle

The same letter is missing from the words in each set. Write the missing letters in the shapes. Then use those letters to solve Farmer Pete's riddle: What did the baby corn say to its mother?

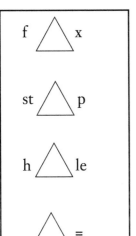

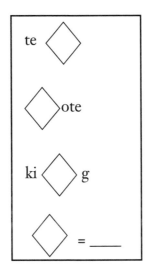

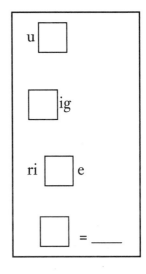

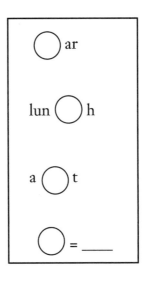

Answer: I want □ △ □ ○ △ ⬡ ◇ !

Answer on page 182.

63

Name That Homonym

Homonyms are words that sound alike but are spelled differently. For example, **ATE** and **EIGHT** are homonyms. Choose the correct homonym to complete each sentence.

1. One plus one equals _____ .

   two   **too**

2. A cub grows up to be a _____ .

   bare   **bear**

3. My house is over _____ .

   their   **there**

4. I like to go to the butcher to buy _____ .

   meat   **meet**

5. I asked the barber to cut my _____ .

   hare   **hair**

6. Can you speak up? I can't _____ .

   here   **hear**

7. To bake a cake you need _____ .

   flower   **flour**

8. A male pig is a _____ .

   bore   **boar**

Answers on page 182.

Brain Food

Help the little fish swim through the brain coral so he can get away from the bigger fish.

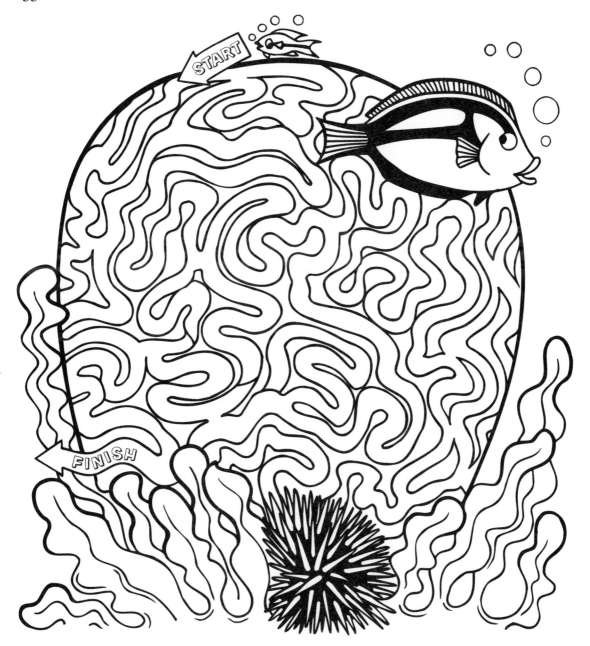

START

FINISH

Answer on page 182.

Wacky Wordies

These word pictures are a wacky way to show a word or phrase. Study each one, and write the words or phrase on the blank lines.

1. PANDA = _____

2. [tide] = _____

3. RETRAUQ = _____

4. [ ] get = _____

5. F I L L = _____

6. [NO / RIGHT] = _____

Answers on page 182.

What Comes Before?

Unscramble and complete this riddle by writing the letter of the alphabet that comes BEFORE each of these letters (A=Z, B=A, C=B, etc.).

Question:

— — — —   — —   — — —
X I B U   E P   Z P V

— — — —   —   — — — —
D B M M   B   T P O H

— — — — —   — — — — ?
B C P V U   D B S T

Answer:

—
— — — —   — — — — !
B   D B S   U V O F

Answer on page 182.

Fishy Squares

How many squares are in each fish below? Be careful! Some squares might be hidden.

1.

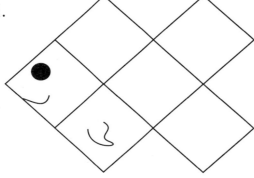

_____ squares

2.

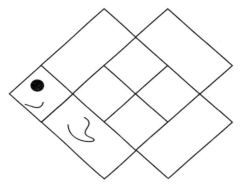

_____ squares

3.

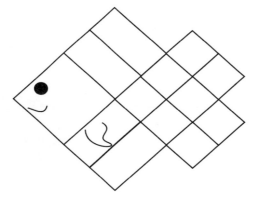

_____ squares

Answers on page 182.

Letters in Colors A

One letter was added to each word in Column 1 to make a new word in Column 2. Find the added letter, and write it in Column 3. Then read down to find a color.

Column 1	Column 2	Column 3
RAN	RANG	_____
TIP	TRIP	_____
HAT	HEAT	_____
BAR	BEAR	_____
EAT	NEAT	_____

Letters in Colors B

Now find another color.

Column 1	Column 2	Column 3
EARL	EARLY	_____
TWIN	TWINE	_____
BACK	BLACK	_____
PEAR	PEARL	_____
PINT	POINT	_____
OMEN	WOMEN	_____

Answers on page 182.

Crazy Circles

Only 2 of these circles are the same. Look carefully to find them. Draw a line connecting the 2 circles.

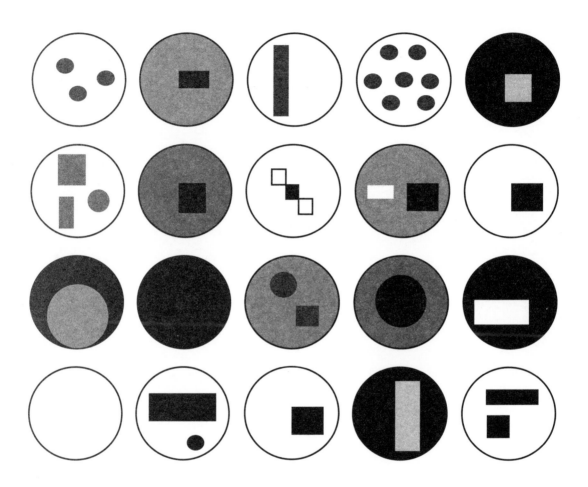

Answer on page 182.

Take Note

The grid contains all 16 words in the word list. Words may run forward or backward, up or down, or diagonally, but they are always in a straight line. When you've found all the words, read the leftover letters from left to right, top to bottom to learn why the hip-hop star went into the CD shop.

Word List

Country

Disco

Funk

Golden oldie

Gospel

Hip-hop

House

Jazz

Latin

Mood

Opera

Reggae

Rock

Soul

Swing

Techno

```
                              G
                              O  N
                              L     I
                              D        W
                              E           S
                              N           O
                              O           U
                              L           L
                              D        T
                 R  A  O  I
              O  M  P  R  E  H
           C  N  I  O  A  E  I  C
        K  K  H  U  G  O  S  P  E  L
        P  S  C  G  O  F  D  H  O  M
        E  R  E  S  U  O  H  O  A  P
        Y  R  T  N  U  O  C  P  Z  P
           I  K  N  G  S  P  Z  A
           P  N  I  T  A  L
           D  E  J  R
```

Answer: _____

Answers on page 182.

A Cagey Riddle

Write the answer to each clue in the boxes below. When you read down the first column of letters, the answer to this riddle will be revealed: What did the ribcage say to the heart?

1. Cannot be done

2. A carnivorous bird

3. Opposite of dead

4. Disappear suddenly

5. To vote into office

6. The day before today

7. Smell or scent

8. One of a kind

9. Where a king and queen live

10. Watch carefully

11. Most brides wear one of these

12. Opposite of full

13. Trees and teeth have these

14. Wicked

15. To pull something along the ground

Answer: _____ !

Answers on page 182.

Baker Bob's Puzzling Pies

Help Baker Bob cut his pies. The pieces do not have to be the same shape or size.

1. Draw 3 straight lines across the pie to make 6 pieces.

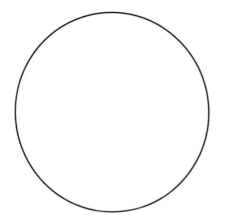

2. Draw 3 straight lines across the pie to make 7 pieces.

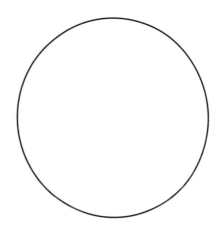

3. Draw 4 straight lines across the pie to make 9 pieces.

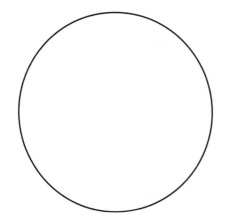

4. Draw 4 straight lines across the pie to make 10 pieces.

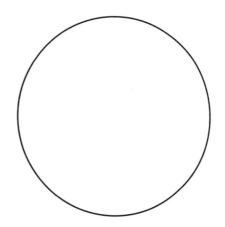

Answers on page 183.

Half-Word Puzzle

Use the pictures to fill in the across blanks, then use the clues to fill in the down blanks.

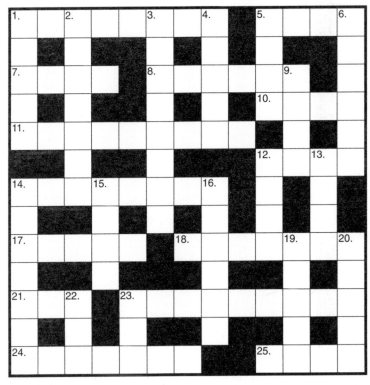

ACROSS

1.

5.

7.

8.

10.

11.

12.

14.

17.

18.

21.

23.

24.

25.

DOWN

1. Coins worth 10 cents
2. Halloween's month
3. The holes in your nose
4. What you think with
5. Not quiet

6. Kind of art you might hang on a wall
9. Opposite of west
12. Gets in a chair
13. Pain
14. Animal that's a lot like a bison
15. Take a _ _ _ _ (get clean)
16. Pirates fight with them
19. Candy that people pull
20. "_ _ _ _ _ are red, violets are blue . . ."
22. Have a meal
23. Move like a rabbit

Answers on page 183.

By the Numbers

Each answer in this quiz is a num ber from 1 to 10. **Hint:** Every number is used exactly once.

1. _____ days in a week

2. _____ strikes and you're out in baseball

3. _____ dimes in a U.S. dollar

4. _____ consonants in "Butterfingers"

5. _____ scarecrow(s) in *The Wizard of Oz*

6. _____ arms on an octopus

7. _____ sides on a single die

8. _____ Great Lakes in the United States

9. _____ tires on a motorcycle

10. _____ main points on a compass

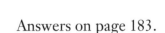

Answers on page 183.

Take Me to Your Mummy

He's tricked or treated, and now he can't get out of his costume! Help this mummy unravel his wrappings so he can dig into his candy.

Answer on page 183.

Missing Shapes

Fill in the grid by drawing circles, triangles, hearts, and diamonds.

Follow these rules:

1. No shape may appear twice in the same row.

2. No shape may appear twice in the same column.

3. No shape may appear twice in a diagonal row that goes from one corner of the grid to the other.

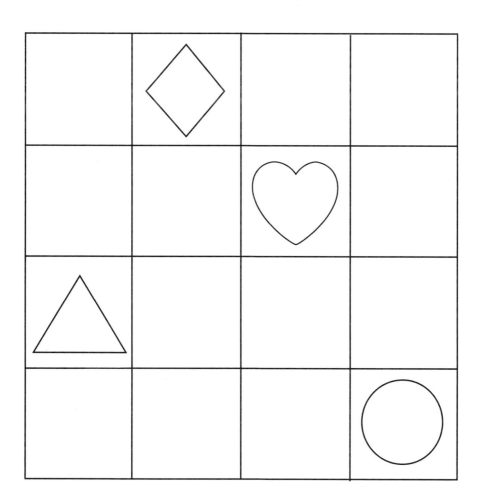

Answer on page 183.

What Am I?

Here's a countdown of 10 statements about a thing. How many will it take you to figure out what it is? Write your answer in the blank at the bottom of the page when you think you've figured it out.

10. I'm useful to both boys and girls.

9. I can be used at home and at school.

8. I'm usually made of plastic.

7. I can be carried in a purse or pocket.

6. Hold me in your hand to use me.

5. I have teeth, but I don't bite.

4. I'm good for a part, but not a part in a play.

3. I can be found in a barbershop.

2. I'm used in your hair.

1. My name rhymes with "home."

Answer: _____

Answer on page 183.

Bottles, Bottles Everywhere (Part 1)

How good is your memory? Take 2 minutes to study the laundry room below. Then turn the page for a quiz on what you've seen.

79

Bottles, Bottles Everywhere (Part II)

*(Do **not** read this page until you have read page 79!)*

Below are 10 bottles—6 of them appeared on page 79, and 4 are new ones. Using your memory, circle the bottles that you saw in the laundry room.

Answers on page 183.

Call a Doctor

Unscramble the following letters to come up with real words. Use the clues to help you.

1. ENIDEMCI _____
(makes you feel better)

2. NAYHICPIS _____
(a doctor)

3. OTHASPLI _____
(where doctors work)

4. SEADIES _____
(medical condition)

5. ERUNS _____
(this person takes your temperature)

6. GABDEAN _____
(covering for wounds)

7. LENEDE _____
(used to give a shot)

Answers on page 183.

Fun with Leftover Letters

Cross out every letter that appears 5 times. Then write the remaining letters from left to right and top to bottom in the lines at the bottom of the page to answer this riddle: What do you call a person who can't flip pancakes?

R	E	A	S	N	T	F	C
B	W	R	U	L	B	S	M
C	I	G	E	M	W	T	E
R	U	S	M	C	P	G	B
G	F	T	E	U	W	N	R
T	C	S	N	M	U	B	L
W	N	B	O	G	S	T	M
R	G	E	W	U	C	P	N

Answer: ____   ____ ____ ____ ____   ____ ____ ____ ____

Answer on page 183.

Look for These C's

How many things can you find that start with the letter **C?** Finding 20 would be COOL. Finding 25 would be COMPLETELY amazing!

Answers on page 183.

Tricky 2's

Add a math symbol between each number 2 so that the equation adds up to 5.
Hint: One of the math symbols is used twice.

$$2 \underline{\hspace{1cm}} 2 \underline{\hspace{1cm}} 2 \underline{\hspace{1cm}} 2 \underline{\hspace{1cm}} 2 = 5$$

Magic Square

Use the numbers 7, 8, 9, 13, 14, and 15 so that each row, column, and diagonal adds up to 33.

10			33
	11		33
		12	33
33	33	33	33

Answers on page 184.

Are You Packed Yet?

Circle the 15 words related to a beach vacation hidden in the suitcase-shape grid below. Words may run forward or backward and up or down, but they are always in a straight line. We found the word **Sandals** to get you started.

Word List

Bathing suit

Beach towel

Camera

Doll

Hats

Money

Pail

Pants

~~Sandals~~

Shorts

Sunglasses

Sunscreen

T-shirt

Tank top

Toys

```
            B     B     S
            A           U
            T           N
B   E   C   H   A   G   D   R   T
E   P   A   I   L   L   O   E   O
A  (S   A   N   D   A   L   S)  Y
C   C   F   G   U   S   L   U   S
H   A   T   S   L   S   N   N   H
T   M   A   U   O   E   T   S   O
O   E   N   I   T   S   O   C   R
W   R   K   T   S   H   I   R   T
E   A   T   G   E   T   A   E   S
L   S   O   U   M   O   N   E   Y
N   B   P   A   N   T   S   N   U
    R                       N
```

Answers on page 184.

Black and White All Over

Whoops! Our picture got scrambled! To put it back together, copy each box into the empty grid (the letters and numbers tell you which box to fill in). We've done the first one for you.

	1	2	3	4
A				
B				
C				
D				

Answer on page 184.

Heartbreaker Challenge

Without lifting your pencil, connect the 9 hearts by drawing only 4 lines!

Answer on page 184.

Lend Me an Ear

This puzzle is a little EAR-y. Fill in the blanks to form words that contain the letters **E, A,** and **R.** The clues in parentheses will help you in your sEARch.

1. ____ E A R (animal that likes honey)

2. ____ E A R ____ (listened to)

3. ____ E A R ____ (rips)

4. ____ E A R ____ (precious jewel)

5. ____ E A R ____ (hair on Santa's chin)

6. E A R ____ ____ (ahead of time)

7. ____ E A R ____ ____ (suit in a deck of cards)

8. ____ E A R ____ ____ ____ (closest)

9. ____ E A R ____ ____ ____ (afraid)

10. ____ E A R ____ ____ ____ ____ (studying in school)

11. ____ ____ ____ ____ E A R (fuzzy in understanding)

12. ____ ____ ____ ____ E A R (kind of submarine; uses the same letters as #11)

13. ____ ____ ____ ____ ____ E A R (name on a blimp or brand of tires)

14. ____ ____ E A R ____ ____ ____ ____ (chewing gum flavor)

15. ____ ____ ____ ____ ____ ____ E A R (vanish into thin air)

Answers on page 184.

Spell It Out

Write the name of each object pictured. When you're finished, the letters in the boxes—read from top to bottom—will spell out the name of a U.S. state.

State: _____

Answers on page 184.

Mega Matchup

How quickly can you find the 3 pairs of matching squares in this puzzle? Look closely—some squares are turned sideways.

Answers on page 184.

91

At the Park

Change 1 letter in each word to make a list of things in the picture below.

1. true _____

2. glass _____

3. sting _____

4. glide _____

5. beach _____

6. bath _____

7. luck _____

8. bond _____

9. bite _____

10. slower _____

Answers on page 184.

Sum—mertime

A question is hidden in these math problems. Solve the problems, then write the sums in order from lowest to highest on the top line of blanks below. On the second line of blanks, write the letter from the matching box. We hope you'll answer "Yes" to the question that appears.

$25 + 3 + 6 =$ ☐ H

$7 + 6 =$ ☐ O

$4 + 12 =$ ☐ I

$11 + 10 + 9 + 8 =$ ☐ A

$44 + 7 + 30 =$ ☐ M

$52 + 46 =$ ☐ U

$33 + 27 =$ ☐ E

$18 + 1 =$ ☐ D

$9 + 6 + 8 =$ ☐ Y

$5 + 5 + 5 =$ ☐ D

$1 + 2 + 3 + 4 =$ ☐ S

$46 + 27 =$ ☐ S

$33 + 3 + 63 =$ ☐ N

$28 + 35 + 13 + 13 =$ ☐ F

$11 + 19 =$ ☐ U

$16 + 10 =$ ☐ O

$23 + 41 + 15 =$ ☐ U

$20 + 7 + 18 =$ ☐ V

_ _ _ _ _ _ _ _ _ _ _ _ _ _ _ _

_ _ _ _ _ _ _ _ _ _ _ _ _ _ _ _?

Answers on page 184.

93

Going in Circles

These words represent 8 things that go in circles. For each circle, begin at 1 letter, and read the word either clockwise or counterclockwise.

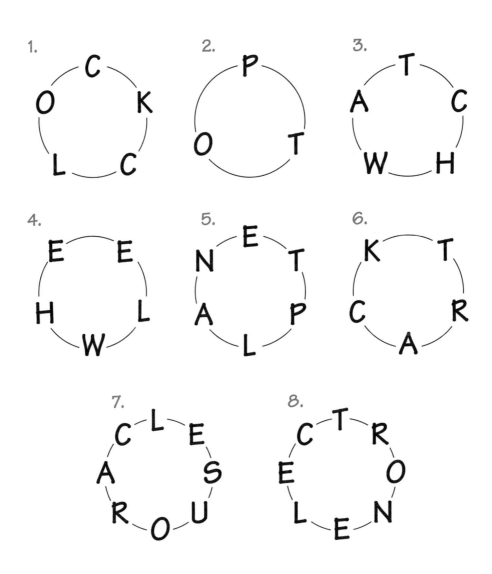

Answers on page 184.

Make-a-Word

Take a word from Column 1, add a word from Column 2, then add a word from Column 3 to form a common word. Write the new word on the blank space. Be careful! Some words can be used with more than 1 other word. Each word should be used exactly once.

Column 1	Column 2	Column 3	Word
AM	A	ACHE	1. _____
CAB	AD	AD	2. _____
CAN	ART	AL	3. _____
CAP	FOR	ATE	4. _____
CAT	GET	BALL	5. _____
DO	HE	HER	6. _____
HE	I	LOG	7. _____
IN	IT	MAT	8. _____
ME	ON	MED	9. _____
NO	OR	NET	10. _____
RED	NON	OW	11. _____
TO	PUT	TIME	12. _____

Answers on page 184.

W Is for Watching and Waiting

How many things can you find that start with the letter **W**? Finding 20 would be WONDERFUL. Finding 25 would be WELL DONE indeed!

Answers on page 185.

Kitchen Mix-Up

Lenny and Jenny got their letters mixed up! Help them unscramble each word to make new words for things that are usually found in the kitchen.

1. top _____

2. nap _____

3. blow _____

4. gum _____

5. votes _____

6. skin _____

7. bleat _____

8. snoop _____

9. pleat _____

10. owlet _____

Answers on page 185.

Road Sign Shapes

The writing from these road signs has disappeared—can you tell what each one means just from its shape?

1. _____ 2. _____ 3. _____ 4. _____

5. _____ 6. _____ 7. _____ 8. _____

Answers on page 185.

Area Code

The cell phones below are displaying a hidden message, but because reception isn't good in this area, the message has broken up. To find out what the message is, first write down the letters displayed on all the cell phones with an antenna on the left side. Then write down all the letters on the cell phones that have a striped rectangle around the message box. Then write down all the others. You should always read the letters from left to right and top to bottom.

Answer: _____

_____!

Answer on page 185.

Anthony's Ant Words

Anthony Ant collects words that contain the letters **A, N,** and **T.** Help him out by filling in the blanks to form words that contain these letters.

1. A living thing that is not an animal   ____ ____ A N T

2. Clothes that are worn from the waist down   ____ A N T ____

3. A fairy-tale character who is very large   ____ ____ A N T

4. A deer's horns   A N T ____ ____ ____ ____

5. To have a desire for   ____ A N T

6. To slope away from a straight line   ____ ____ A N T

7. To give or allow   ____ ____ A N T

8. A leopard with a black coat   ____ A N T ____ ____ ____

9. A long, thin feeler on the head of an insect   A N T ____ ____ ____ ____

10. An outburst of bad temper   ____ A N T ____ ____ ____

Answers on page 185.

Race Through Space

Our space friends are late for a picnic on Pluto! Help them navigate through the solar system and get there as fast as possible.

Answer on page 185.

2 Times 2

The words below begin and end with the same 2 letters in the same order, but we've left them out. Use the clues in parentheses to help you fill in the blanks.

1. ____ ____ O R ____ ____ (first U.S. president's name)

2. ____ ____ A ____ ____ (home of football's Dolphins)

3. ____ ____ C I ____ ____ (make a choice)

4. ____ ____ O T O G R A ____ ____ (picture made by a camera)

5. ____ ____ C A P ____ ____ (prison breakouts)

6. ____ ____ R A I G H T E ____ ____ (least crooked)

Answers on page 185.

Rest Stop

The drawing on this page is really 3 puzzles in 1! Test your powers of observation by completing the following activities.

1. Circle 5 things that begin with the letter **R**.

2. Put an X through 5 things that are wrong with this picture.

3. Find 6 hidden letters in this picture. Unscramble the letters to form a word that describes what you have after visiting a rest stop.

Answer: _____

Answers on page 185.

GO FOR THE BURN

Know Your Numbers

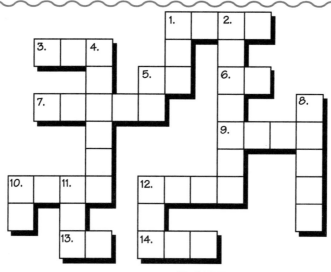

ACROSS

1. The year the United States was born

3. The number of days in a year

5. The number of yards in 192 feet

6. The number of days in 8 weeks

7. The number that comes after 40,079

9. The number of seconds in 1 hour

10. The number of feet in a mile

12. 2,222÷2

13. 9×9+9

14. The number of legs on 50 spiders

DOWN

1. The number of cookies in 12 dozen

2. 7,654,000+321

4. Half a million

5. The number of months in 5 years

8. 3,401×3

10. The number of nickels needed to make $2.75

11. 135+714

12. The number of tires on 26 cars

Answers on page 185.

Similar Sounds

Homophones are words that sound alike but are spelled differently. Fill in the blank spaces with words that are homophones of each other. We've done the first one for you. Note that sentences 14 and 15 contain 3 homophones.

1. For a snack I <u>ATE</u> at least <u>**EIGHT**</u> of the donuts.

2. I _____ a raffle prize of exactly _____ dollar.

3. At the party I didn't _____ anybody, and _____ one spoke to me.

4. Let's _____ at the butcher shop to buy some _____.

5. After taking off my glasses, _____ got some dust in my left _____.

6. Do you know the _____ to _____ things on this scale?

7. The wind _____ so hard and was so cold that my lips turned _____.

8. A _____ for the boat was on _____ at the store.

9. The _____ of the Round Table spent a few _____ sleeping at the inn.

10. I paid the _____ for the taxi ride to the state _____.

11. I _____ in the newspaper about a protest in Moscow's _____ Square.

12. I wasn't sure of the amount, but I _____ how much the hotel _____ paid for his room.

13. I brought a _____ to water the garden and some _____ to dig it up.

14. Through the mail, I _____ 20 dollars and one _____ for a perfume with a wonderful _____.

15. On the high _____, the pirate captain likes to _____ ships right after he _____ them through his spyglass.

Answers on page 185.

1 Word + 1 Word = 1 Word

A compound word is a word made from 2 smaller words. Scarecrow is a compound word. SCARE+CROW=SCARECROW. Match a word from Column 1 to a word in Column 2 to form a compound word. Be careful: Some words may have more than one match!

Column 1	Column 2
CROSS	HOPPER
WATER	LIGHT
HOME	BALL
POP	END
BASE	WORK
RAIN	CROW
FLASH	COAT
NOTE	WALK
GRASS	BOOK
SCARE	FALL
WEEK	CORN

Answers on page 185.

3-Letter Challenge

Fill in the boxes so that each vertical column contains a 3-letter word. Use the letters in the clouds to help you. If you complete each set correctly, the letters in each center row will spell the name of an animal.

1.

A	F	B	N	A	B
E	G	E	W	E	G

2.

A	D	T	H	I	O	B
E	T	Y	D	L	D	T

3.

E	H	T	A	L	A	A
F	N	N	E	P	T	D

4.

P	A	T	S	T	F	E	I
G	L	N	Y	E	N	D	S

Answers on page 186.

Inside the Opposites

Fill in each set of blanks with the word that means the opposite of the word listed. If you choose the correct word, the new word will have the meaning of the words in parentheses.

1. down   P ___ ___ P Y (a young dog)

2. come   ___ ___ O S E (a water bird)

3. high   P I L ___ ___ ___ (a soft cushion)

4. in   S P ___ ___ ___ (a teapot's narrow opening)

5. open   ___ ___ ___ ___ ___ T (a storage room)

6. cold   ___ ___ ___ E L (a building for guests)

7. sick   S ___ ___ ___ ___ (to grow in size)

8. slow   E N ___ ___ ___ ___ (to attach)

9. bottom   ___ ___ ___ P L E (to cause to fall)

10. out   S H R ___ ___ K (to become smaller)

11. poor   E N ___ ___ ___ ___ (to improve)

12. happy   ___ ___ ___ D L E (seat on a horse)

13. new   B ___ ___ ___ (brave)

14. heavy   D E ___ ___ ___ ___ ___ (joy or pleasure)

15. over   T H ___ ___ ___ ___ ___ (rumbling sound that follows lightning)

Answers on page 186.

Basketball Signs

"Hoop" it up with this brain-building sports puzzle. See if you can match the list of basketball referee signals with the appropriate drawing.

Signals

  Score

  Start the clock

  Stop the clock

  Technical foul

  Traveling

1. _____

2. _____

3. _____

4. _____

5. _____

Answers on page 186.

Pairs to Compare

An **analogy** is a comparison between 2 pairs of items. The first pair of items is related in the same way as the second pair. For example: **WRITER** is to **BOOK** as **ARTIST** is to **PAINTING.** Use the words in the box below to finish each analogy. (We've added an extra word to the box to make it tricky!)

cotton	floor	boat	thermometer
down	glove	sled	vegetable
eleventh	hat	swimming	water
		taste	

1. TIME is to CLOCK as TEMPERATURE is to _____.

2. BLOUSE is to SHIRT as BONNET is to _____.

3. HORSE is to CARRIAGE as DOG is to _____.

4. BIRD is to FLYING as FISH is to _____.

5. WALLPAPER is to WALL as RUG is to _____.

6. NOSE is to SMELL as TONGUE is to _____.

7. CAR is to LAND as BOAT is to _____.

8. HEAD is to HELMET as HAND is to _____.

9. SECOND is to THIRD as TENTH is to _____.

10. ASTRONAUT is to SPACESHIP as SAILOR is to _____.

11. NONSENSE is to SENSE as UP is to _____.

12. APPLE is to FRUIT as CORN is to _____.

Answers on page 186.

Avalanche Maze

Follow the path of footprints in this maze to help the mapmaker get to the cabin. Watch out for false leads! **Hint:** Use your pencil to trace along the footprints so you don't accidentally skip to another set of tracks.

Answer on page 186.

Number Facts

Can you figure out which words are missing from each number fact? Use the capital letters to help you. Then complete the facts and write them on the lines. The first one is done for you.

1. 12 I in a F   _12 Inches in a Foot_

2. 365 D in a Y   _____

3. 24 H in a D   _____

4. 3 W on a T   _____

5. 52 W in a Y   _____

6. 100 C in a M   _____

7. 4 Q in a G   _____

8. 16 O in a P   _____

9. 60 M in an H   _____

10. 10 Y in a D   _____

11. 26 L of the A   _____

12. 8 T on an O   _____

13. 4 Q in a D   _____

14. 60 S in a M   _____

15. 100 Y in a C   _____

16. 50 S on the U.S. F   _____

Answers on page 186.

What's Wrong in Time?

Take a look at this picture, and you'll see what it was like to be a kid living during the colonial days of George Washington. Everything here looks just like it did more than 200 years ago. But wait...how did that get there? It seems our artist made a mistake, accidentally adding a few things that weren't yet invented in 1776. Find 10 out-of-time objects.

Answers on page 186.

PANdemonium

Fill in the blanks to make words that start with the word **PAN.**

1. You eat these for breakfast

   PAN_____

2. This animal is native to China

   PAN_____

3. A type of flower

   PAN_____

4. Where you put boxes of food at home

   PAN_____

5. Country in Central America

   PAN_____

6. A type of wild feline

   PAN_____

7. Article of clothing

   PAN_____

8. Extreme anxiety

   PAN_____

Answers on page 186.

Eagle Eyes

Here's a riddle: Who can raise things without lifting them? To find the answer, look at every small grid below. One letter of the alphabet has been left out of each grid. Write the missing letter on each line. Then read the letters from 1 to 7 to find the 2-word answer.

F	W	M	V	B
J	Q	C	N	G
R	D	L	U	X
E	P	I	O	Y
K	S	T	Z	H

1. _____

E	H	P	Q	G
S	D	T	W	K
U	X	C	J	O
Z	V	N	M	B
F	Y	I	L	A

7. _____

E	T	P	V	F
X	J	U	W	Y
Z	Q	I	R	D
C	H	O	N	B
G	S	K	L	M

3. _____

C	M	L	K	J
N	B	X	Y	I
O	W	A	Z	H
P	V	U	D	G
Q	S	T	R	F

6. _____

Z	U	W	C	L
Y	V	B	J	K
T	A	M	O	D
S	X	N	E	I
Q	P	F	G	H

4. _____

E	L	A	S	F
Z	K	G	U	B
W	V	H	J	T
C	R	I	N	O
X	P	Q	Y	D

5. _____

Y	G	R	V	W
H	X	I	M	D
T	N	C	L	Z
B	S	K	U	O
A	Q	J	P	E

2. _____

Answer on page 186.

Christmas Clues

Read the clues, and write the correct word in the blanks to figure out the answer to this following riddle: What do you get when you cross a snowman with a vampire? The answer will be in the colored boxes.

1. ___ ___ ___ ___ ___ ___ ___

2. ___ ___ ___ ___ ___ ___

3. ___ ___ ___ ___ ___ ___

4. ___ ___ ___ ___ ___ ___ ___

5. ___ ___ ___ ___ ___ ___ ___ ___ ___

6. ___ ___ ___

7. ___ ___ ___ ___

8. ___ ___ ___ ___

9. ___ ___ ___ ___

1. Famous snowman

2. Songs sung around Christmastime

3. Reindeer with a red nose

4. Left under a Christmas tree by Santa

5. Items hung on a Christmas tree

6. Scrooge says, "_____, humbug!"

7. The color of snow

8. He delivers presents on a sleigh

9. Winged creature placed atop a Christmas tree

Answer: _____

Answers on page 186.

Country Balloons

In each balloon, there is the name of a country, but it is missing 1 letter. Write the country name on the blank, and write the missing letter next to each name. Then rearrange those missing letters to spell another country.

1. _____

2. _____

3. _____

4. _____

5. _____

6. _____

7. _____

8. _____

9. _____

1.

2.

3.

4.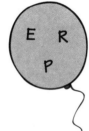

5.

6.

7.

8.

9.

Answer: _____

Answers on page 186.

OR Bits

Place these 20 words containing the letters OR into the grid so that they intersect as in a crossword. When you are done, all the words will have been used exactly once. **Hint:** Start with the 9-letter word.

3 Letters
nor

ore

4 Letters
form

port

5 Letters
favor

lords

major

north

order

score

torso

6 Letters
chorus

errors

forest

horror

meteor

stormy

7 Letters
corners

shortly

9 Letters
doorbells

Answers on page 186.

State Match

Can you match the name of the state with its shape? Sound easy? Well, you'd better be careful—some of the states are shown sideways, upside-down, or even reversed, as if you were looking at them in a mirror! Write your answers on the lines.

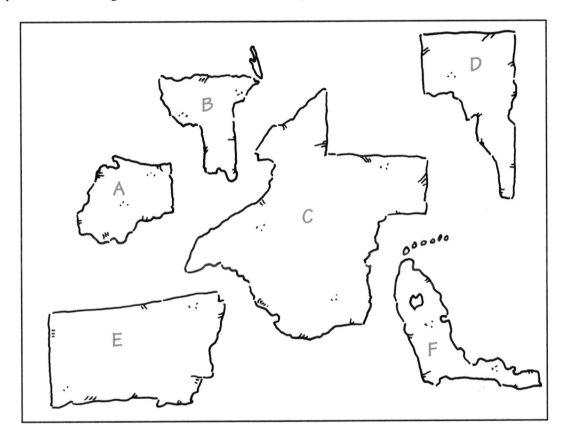

A. _____   D. _____

B. _____   E. _____

C. _____   F. _____

Answers on page 187.

Spell It Out

First, identify each picture. Then, spell out each word and add and subtract letters as indicated. (The letters you subtract won't necessarily be in order.) If you do the puzzle correctly, you will spell the name of a country.

_____

_____

_____

Answer on page 187.

Anatonyms Challenge

An **anatonym** is a verb that also names a part of the body. For example, you're using an anatonym when you say, "Please **HAND** me that book." Write the anatonym that completes each sentence below. Use the words in the box to help you.

arm	foot	finger	face	mouth
eye	elbow	nose	skin	shoulder

1. We always _____ the camera when we get our picture taken.

2. The Turners _____ the bill whenever they invite us out to eat.

3. The cat seemed to _____ the mouse's every movement.

4. Brian thinks it's unfair that he has to _____ the blame for the broken window.

5. The soldiers had to _____ themselves for battle.

6. I saw Mrs. Lee _____ the silk cloth gently.

7. The detective said he would _____ around for any possible clues.

8. Arnie tried to _____ his way to the front of the line.

9. If you fall on the pavement, you might _____ your knee.

10. Some of the choir members had sore throats, so they could only _____ the words.

Answers on page 187.

Geography Quiz

How well do you know world geography? See how many of these questions you can answer on your own. If you have trouble, consult an atlas.

1. Can you name all the continents? _____

_____

Which one is the largest? _____

2. Can you name all the Great Lakes? _____

Which one is the biggest? _____

3. Can you name the people carved on Mount Rushmore? _____

_____

What do they all have in common? _____

4. What were the last two states to be added to the United States?

_____

5. Where are the highest and lowest points located in the United States?

_____

Bonus: Where in the United States can you stand in four states at once?

_____

Answers on page 187.

Missing Shapes

Fill in the grid by drawing squares, circles, triangles, hearts, and diamonds.

Follow these rules:

1. No shape may appear twice in the same row.

2. No shape may appear twice in a column.

3. No shape may appear twice in a diagonal row that goes from one corner to the other.

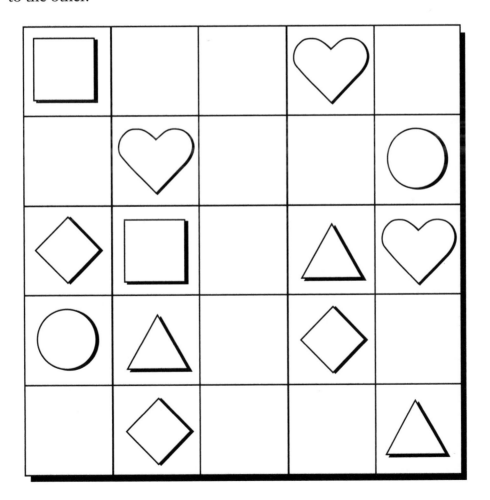

Answer on page 187.

Sentence Riddles

Use the clues to "read" each phrase below. Then write the familiar phrase on the lines.

1. THESINGINGRAIN _____

2. ii   ii
   ( )   ( )   _____

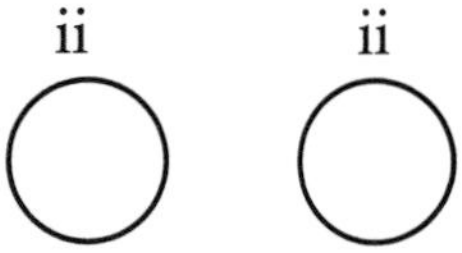

3. [   ] THINK   _____

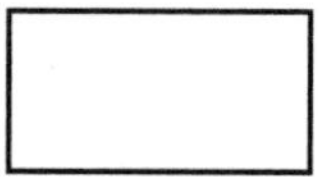

4. WATER
   ~~~~~
   UNDER   _____

5. JACK   _____

6. T I R E   _____

7. FACE   _____

8. (GHORSING circular)   _____

Answers on page 187.

The Professor's Lists

Professor Whiz loves to make lists! Last week, he started writing number words on a sheet of paper. He began with one. Then he wrote two, three, four, five, and so on. He kept writing the number words in order until he came to one that had the letter **A**. He wrote that word, and then he stopped. "I'm finally done!" he said.

A. What was the last number word on the professor's list?

_____

Later, Professor Whiz started a list like this:

$1+2=3$

$1+2+3=6$

$1+2+3+4=10$

$1+2+3+4+5=15$

$1+2+3+4+5+6=21$

B. What sum will the Professor get when he adds 10 numbers together?

_____

Answers on page 187.

Restaurant Scene

It's 3 puzzles in 1! Look at the picture below, and complete the following activities:

1. Find 5 things that are wrong with this picture.

2. Circle 5 things that begin with the letter **C.**

3. There are 6 hidden letters in this drawing. Find them, then unscramble them to form a word that describes the restaurant's customers.

Answers on page 187.

Mystery Animals

Write the name of the animal that is described in each clue. Use the words in the box to help you.

duck	raccoon	spider	orangutan
lion	hippopotamus	aardvark	beluga whale
armadillo	camel		

1. This animal's name means "river horse." _____

2. This animal has been called the "king of beasts" because of its strength and beauty. _____

3. This animal is known as the "ship of the desert" because it is used for transporting people and goods. _____

4. Dutch settlers in Africa gave this animal its name, which means "earth pig."

   _____

5. In the Malay language, this animal's name means "man of the forest."

   _____

6. The meaning of this animal's name is "little man in armor."

   _____

7. Because of its loud whistles and bell-like calls, this animal has been called a "sea canary." _____

8. This animal's name comes from an old English word meaning "spinner."

   _____

9. Native Americans named this animal with a word meaning "scratcher."

   _____

10. This animal's name comes from an old English word meaning "diver."

   _____

Answers on page 187.

Once Around the Big Block

Use the clues to fill in the blanks around the block. Start each word in the same space as its clue number. Each word will start with the last 2 letters of the word that comes before it. When you get to a corner, follow the direction of the arrow.

Clues

1. Tank in which to keep fish

2. Person who calls balls and strikes

3. One of the two major political parties in the United States

4. Joint near your foot

5. Drink you might sell at a stand

6. Person who cleans your teeth

7. Ohio or Texas, for example

8. Awful

9. Strap for holding onto a dog

10. Short version of the name of a really big pro basketball star

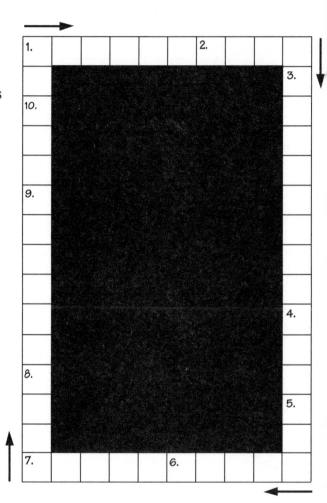

Answers on page 187.

What in the World?

An alien has dropped into your living room from outer space. She doesn't know anything about life on Earth and is confused about holidays. Fill her in on some holiday facts. When you're finished, read the circled letters for a special message to the alien.

1. The first day of the year __ __ ◯ __ __ __ __ ' __ __ __ __

2. The day you look for bunnies and eggs __ __ __ __ ◯ __

3. The day to celebrate work ◯ __ __ __ __ __ __ __

4. When we sing carols and hope for snow ◯ __ __ __ __ __ __ __ __

5. When things go "Boo!" in the night __ __ __ __ ◯ __ __ __ __

6. The day we remember those who have passed away

    __ __ ◯ __ __ __ __ __ __ __ __

7. When we remember our country's leaders

    __ __ ◯ __ __ __ __ __ __ __ ' __ __ __

8. This day is all hearts and flowers ,

    __ __ __ __ __ ◯ __ __ __ __ __ __ __

9. Don't forget your mom on this day __ ◯ __ __ __ __ __ __ __ __

10. The day to celebrate your dad __ __ __ __ ◯ __ __ __ __ __ __

11. It's a great day to be grateful __ __ ◯ __ __ __ __ __ __ __ __ __

12. When we take care of Mother Nature __ __ ◯ __ __ __ __ __

13. Don't forget to wear green on this day ,

    __ ◯. __ __ __ __ __ __ __ __ __ __ __

14. This day is full of parades, picnics, and fireworks

    __ __ __ __ __ ◯ __ __ __ __ __ __

Message:_____!   Answers on page 187.

What a Mess!

It's late and time for bed. But whoa! This room is a mess! Can you help this sleepy kid make it to the bed before she falls asleep?

Answer on page 188.

Number Patterns

Look at the rows of numbers. Each row has its own pattern. Figure out the patterns, and then add 3 more numbers to each row.

1. 12, 23, 34, 45, _____, _____, _____

2. 0, 1, 3, 6, 10, 15, _____, _____, _____

3. 19, 28, 37, 46, 55, _____, _____, _____

4. 0, 5, 4, 9, 8, 13, 12, _____, _____, _____

5. 1, 1, 2, 4, 3, 9, 4, 16, _____, _____, _____

6. 0, 1, 1, 2, 3, 5, 8, 13, _____, _____, _____

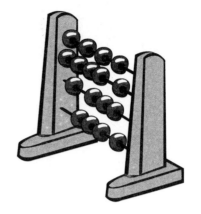

Now look at the numbers in the boxes below. Explain how they are alike.

7.

36	48
84 24	12
21	63

_____
_____

8.

242	396
187	352
561	264

_____
_____

9.

321	432
975 789	456
543	999

_____
_____

Answers on page 188.

International Signs

These international signs were designed to make travel easier for people from all over the world. Can you guess what each sign means?

1. _____

2. _____

3. _____

4. _____

5. _____

6. _____

7. _____

8. _____

9. _____

10. _____

Answers on page 188.

Fun with Opposites

Fill in each set of blanks with the word that means the opposite of the word listed. If you choose the correct word, the new word will have the meaning of the word(s) in parentheses.

1. go   S H O R T ___ ___ ___ ___ (baseball position)

2. near   ___ ___ ___ M E R (he/she grows crops)

3. young   S ___ ___ ___ I E R (army member)

4. on   ___ ___ ___ E R I N G (church donation)

5. first   P ___ ___ ___ ___ I C (what a flying disc is made of)

6. poor   O S T ___ ___ ___ ___ (big bird that can't fly)

7. wet   L A U N ___ ___ ___ (clothes to wash)

8. high   F ___ ___ ___ E R (tulip or daisy)

9. win   C ___ ___ ___ ___ R (nearer)

10. early   C H O C O ___ ___ ___ ___ (milk shake flavor)

11. soft   O R C ___ ___ ___ ___ (place to grow apples)

12. stand   P O ___ ___ ___ I V E (absolutely sure)

Answers on page 188.

Farmer Green's Veggies

The names of Farmer Green's vegetables make up the puzzle below. Fill in the blanks with the other vegetables and herbs he grows.

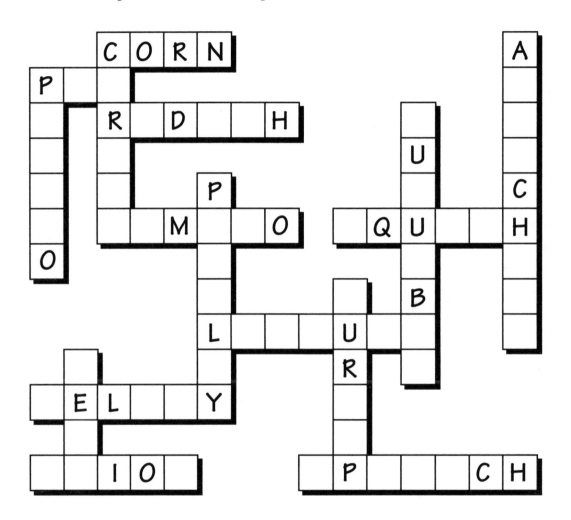

Answers on page 188.

Beam in on B's

This picture is loaded with things that begin with the letter **B**. Finding 30 would be BEAUTIFUL. Finding more than 40 would be BRILLIANT indeed!

Answers on page 188.

135

Where Do They Live?

Draw a line from the circle nearest each animal to the circle nearest its matching habitat. Then look at the letters that have been crossed by the lines. Write the letters in order on the matching numbered lines to find the answer to this riddle: What do you call pigs who write letters to each other?

polar bear	①	M			◯ savanna
lion	②	P	R	E	◯ ocean
toucan	③			P	◯ desert
whale	④		A		◯ pond
camel	⑤	O	N		◯ arctic regions
bighorn sheep	⑥		S		◯ rain forest
frog	⑦	B	L		◯ mountain

Answer: ___ ___ ___   ___ ___ ___ ___
        1   2   3   4   5   6   7

Answers on page 188.

NOW YOU'RE SHAKING AND BAKING!

Follow the Arrows

The clues for this puzzle appear in the grid. Enter the answers in the directions of the arrows.

It's made of links	You take aspirin for it	Not to mention	"What time ___?"	Tidy	Soup with clams	▼	Big jungle animal	Tehran is its capital	Rant and ___ (act angry)	Building for tools
►					Thin items in a brush	►				
"So what ___ is new?"	►				TV star ___ Winfrey	►				
It's next to Europe	►				Use a loom	►				
Finished a lower-case i	►						Mr. Flanders on TV	►		
It helps pay for college		That girl	Fruits from Florida	___ Angeles	Turn over ___ leaf		Cocker ___ (dog)	Red meat	Frozen cubes	Ball-point ___
►										
Wading bird	►				Walk back and forth	►				
Rub out	►				Last word in a prayer	►				
Part of a chicken	Strike	What the bride says		Owns	"I'll ___ monkey's uncle!"			Prefix meaning "three"	Make a knot	Money in Japan
►					Itty-___	►				
Thought	►				Strange	►				
Throw	►				Not of this planet					

Answers on page 188.

Word Morphs

Ever want to turn something hard into something easy? Or a duck into a swan?
Change 1 letter per line to get the answers. Some letters are provided to help you.

H A R D   D U C K

__ __ R __   __ __ C __

__ A __ __   P __ __ __

__ __ __ E   __ __ __ K

E __ __ __   __ E __ __

E A S Y   __ __ __ N

                                B __ __ __

                                __ E __ __

                                __ __ A __

                                S W A N

Answers on page 189.

Plus or Minus

Fill in the plus or minus symbols to make each number sentence correct.

1. 7 ☐ 2 ☐ 5 = 4

2. 5 ☐ 4 ☐ 8 = 9

3. 1 ☐ 3 ☐ 1 = 3

4. 2 ☐ 4 ☐ 6 = 12

5. 9 ☐ 1 ☐ 2 = 8

6. 8 ☐ 6 ☐ 7 ☐ 1 = 10

7. 3 ☐ 1 ☐ 4 ☐ 5 = 11

8. 4 ☐ 6 ☐ 1 ☐ 2 = 7

9. 6 ☐ 5 ☐ 7 ☐ 1 = 5

10. 9 ☐ 4 ☐ 2 ☐ 3 = 4

Answers on page 189.

Splish Splash

Can you find the 17 differences between the top and the bottom pool scenes?

Answers on page 189.

Terrible 2's

Can you figure out the answer to this tongue-twisting math puzzle? Put on your thinking cap and find out!

Tookey and Toomey are both 2. Tookey has 22 toucans. Toomey has 2 toucans. Tookey gave 2 of his toucans to Toomey on Tuesday, 2 more the next Tuesday, and 2 more the next Tuesday. Tookey loved toucans so much, he went to the toucan store and bought 22 more. Toomey came along and bought 2, too. How many toucans does Tookey have? How many toucans does Toomey have? How many toucans is too many toucans?

Answers on page 189.

Anagram Detective

Every sentence below has anagrams. **Anagrams** are words or phrases that are made by rearranging the letters of another word or phrase. Circle the pair of anagrams in each sentence. (Ignore any punctuation.) The anagrams in the first sentence have been circled for you.

1. Jed's mother was surprised that his (dormitory) was such a (dirty room.)

2. When the schoolmaster entered the classroom, there was complete silence.

3. Some fans insist that Elvis lives and that he is working at a diner in Texas.

4. If the room is completely silent, you will hear nothing even if you listen very carefully.

5. The public art galleries are large picture halls, I bet.

6. I hired the detectives to detect thieves who might enter the shop.

7. Everyone knows that eleven plus two equals twelve plus one.

8. Some might argue that a gentleman is an elegant man.

9. If a decimal point could speak, it might shout, "I'm a dot in place!"

10. During vacation times, I'm not as active as I am at other times of the year.

Answers on page 189.

Now What?

The symbols below are organized in patterns. Can you figure out which symbol comes next? Draw your answers on the blank lines.

1.    _____

2.   _____

3. _____

4. _____

5.   _____

6. _____

Answers on page 189.

Word Trios

Change 1 letter in each of the 3 words in a row to get 3 new words that are related. For example, **ORE, TOO, THREW** becomes **ONE, TWO, THREE.**

1. GLUE, BED, FELLOW   _____

2. PLANT, DRAIN, TAR   _____

3. SHOP, BOOT, BERRY   _____

4. WHOLE, DISH, GRAB   _____

5. FREE, PUSH, GRAMS   _____

6. WEAR, PLUG, GRAVE   _____

7. MOAT, CAT, SWEETER   _____

8. DILL, BALK, POP   _____

9. HUMMER, PAW, FRILL   _____

10. CHAIN, BUNCH, STOOP   _____

11. SHOW, LOOT, FLIPPER   _____

12. DIVER, BAKE, SET   _____

Answers on page 189.

Box by Box

The answer to each of these riddles is in 1 of the grids below, but we're not going to tell you which grid goes with which riddle! To find the answers, start at the circled letter and move up, down, or across 1 box at a time until you have traveled through the whole grid. Do not move diagonally. All the letters will be used; there will be no leftover letters.

1. In what school do you have to drop out in order to graduate?

_____

2. Why did Humpty Dumpty have a great fall?

_____

3. What do you get if you cross a jumbo jet and a kangaroo?

_____

A.

D	A	T
S	B	O
U	A	M
M	R	A
M	O	K
E	F	E
R	P	U

B.

P	A	R
O	L	A
O	H	C
S	C	H
E	T	U

C.

A	M	T
K	E	A
S	S	H
H	O	T
T	R	E
H	O	N
S	P	A
A	P	L

Answers on page 189.

I Love a Parade!

Can you find these 11 items hidden in the parade?

Answers on page 189.

Math Mystery

Grab your calculator, and try this math puzzle on for size. Then share it with your friends!

1. Write down any 3-digit number (the number cannot begin with 0). Write the number down again, so it will be a 6-digit number. For example, if you chose 123 then your number would be 123,123.

2. Divide the 6-digit number by 7. (Don't worry about the remainder; there won't be one.)

3. Next, divide the answer by 11. (Don't worry about the remainder; there won't be one.)

4. Next, divide that answer by 13 (Again: Don't worry about the remainder; there won't be one!)

Do you recognize the number?

Answers on page 189.

Surroundings

Put 1 of the 4-letter words from the Word List into the blank spaces around each letter grouping to make a longer word. Use the clues in parentheses to help you.

Word List				
CORD	FISH	LOVE	PEAR	PURE
DEAL	LARK	MILE	PINT	TILE
DEER	LICK	PANT	PLUM	

1. ___ R O S S W ___ ___ ___ (type of puzzle)

2. ___ A N D M ___ ___ ___ (easily seen object used as a guide)

3. ___ ___ T I E ___ ___ (a doctor's client)

4. ___ L E A S ___ ___ ___ (enjoyment)

5. ___ O O L ___ ___ ___ (silly)

6. ___ I P S T ___ ___ ___ (woman's cosmetic item)

7. ___ ___ S E R A B ___ ___ (very unhappy)

8. ___ ___ C U L I ___ ___ (strange)

9. ___ E P P E R M ___ ___ ___ (gum flavor)

10. ___ ___ A T I N ___ ___ (valuable metal)

11. ___ ___ L I V ___ ___ (distribute, like mail)

12. ___ ___ C I M ___ ___ (point in a number)

13. ___ ___ C O M O T I ___ ___ (part of a train)

14. ___ E X T ___ ___ ___ (fabric)

Answers on page 189.

148

Word Bingo

The challenge in this game is to find which row, column, or corner-to-corner diagonal is the bingo line. First, pick a word on the bingo card. Next, go to the Word Bank to see if you can find a word that will combine with the word on the card to create a compound word or phrase. (For example, WASTE plus BASKET would form WASTEBASKET.) Cross out any words on the card that you've successfully blended. (Each Word Bank word can be used only once per row.) Five words in a row or 4 in a row plus the "Free Space!" wins. There is only 1 winning line.

Word Bank	Register	Cane	Rope
Station	Salad	Rock	Cracker
Court	Print	Cloth	Stone
Capital	Screen	Store	Fly
Officer	Pan	Paste	Carton
Tank	Coaster	Clock	Band
	Suit	Plug	

B	I	N	G	O
MOVIE	MARCHING	HALLOWEEN	SNAP	SPACE
FINGER	OAK	STATE	JUMP	SWORD
ROLLER	POLICE	FREE SPACE!	TENNIS	BOOK
FIRE	BATHING	DOG	CASH	CELL
SHIP	MILK	DRAGON	WASH	TOOTH

Answers on page 190.

Pen Pal Letters

Jill wrote letters to her pen pals who live in different parts of the United States. Just for fun, she added their state abbreviations in her letters. See if you can figure out what those abbreviations are and which states her pen pals live in.

Hope to see you this summer if it's ok with your parents!

1. _____

Well, say hi to everyone. I miss you all!

2. _____

Write or call just so I know how you're doing.

3. _____

Oh, don't forget to write back when you have time.

4. _____

Let us know when your flight gets in so that I can meet you.

5. _____

Tell your brother Al that he can visit us anytime.

6. _____

We'd have visited you on this last trip, but Dad said that his wallet was "mt"!

7. _____

My baby sister was so sad to leave that she cried "Wa!" all the way home.

8. _____

My teacher, Ms. Love, says she's from your home state, too!

9. _____

Answers on page 190.

Check This Out!

Solve this like a normal word search, except that the letters CHECK are always replaced by the symbol √ in the grid; for example, the word CHECKERBOARD appears in the grid as √ERBOARD.

Word List

Annual checkup

Blank check

Bounced check

Checkbook

Checkerboard

Checking account

Check it out

Checklist

Check mark

Checkmate

Checkout counter

Checks and balances

Chinese checkers

Chubby Checker

Double-check

Paycheck

Pick up the check

Rubber check

Spellchecker

Spot check

Traveler's checks

```
T  U  O  T  I  √  C  O  E  T  A  M  √
U  C  H  I  N  E  S  E  √  E  R  S  √
T  √  √  L  A  √  E  R  B  O  A  R  D
R  O  P  I  H  B  √  D  E  N  E  Z  E
A  U  T  O  N  R  I  K  D  √  R  P  C
V  T  U  S  E  G  O  B  L  E  E  U  N
E  C  K  B  I  O  A  L  M  L  √  √  U
L  O  B  R  B  L  E  C  T  B  Y  L  O
E  U  P  √  A  P  √  √  C  U  B  A  B
R  N  J  N  S  M  T  Y  G  O  B  U  G
S  T  C  C  P  O  √  S  A  D  U  N  S
√  E  H  T  P  U  K  C  I  P  H  N  A
S  R  J  S  √  K  N  A  L  B  C  A  T
```

Answers on page 190.

Barbershop Bloopers

Can you find 10 or more errors in this barbershop scene?

Answers on page 190.

Squish—Squash

They may look like nonsense, but the letters below are all hiding something. Each group of letters contains the names of 2 flowers. You can still read each flower in order from left to right, but the letters have all been "squashed" together. For example, you could find both **AZALEA** and **CLOVER** in **AZCALOLEVEAR.** Can you "unsquash" all 20 words?

1. ROIRSIES   _____

2. LDAILISYY   _____

3. TULILLAIPC   _____

4. PAPNOSPYPY   _____

5. VORICOHLIETD   _____

6. BEPGEOTNIUNAIA   _____

7. MADARIFFGOLODIDL   _____

8. GERGARADNIEUMNIA   _____

9. SUBNUFLTOTWEERCURP   _____

10. CADRANDNAETILOINON   _____

Answers on page 190.

Pizza Delivery

Ding-dong! It's the pizza delivery person with 3 pizzas for Pepperoni Pete and his friends, Pepperoni Patty, Pepperoni Phil, and Pepperoni Pablo. Can you figure out how many slices each pepperoni-lover will take from each pizza? You can mark on the pizza drawings if you need help.

Pizza A is cut into 4 slices and has 20 pieces of pepperoni evenly spaced. Pizza B is cut into 6 slices and has 24 pieces of pepperoni evenly spaced. Pizza C is cut into 8 slices and has 16 pieces of pepperoni evenly spaced. Time to eat!

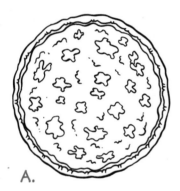 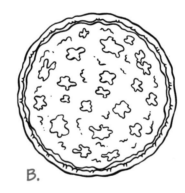 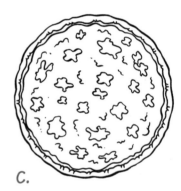

A.   B.   C.

1. Patty wants 3 slices of pizza with 11 pieces of pepperoni.   _____

2. Phil wants 13 pieces of pepperoni but on 3 slices of pizza.   _____

3. Hungry Pablo wants 6 slices of pizza and 12 pieces of pepperoni.   _____

4. Pete wants 14 pieces of pepperoni on 3 slices of pizza.   _____

5. How many slices from each pizza does Pepperoni Pete have left over for tomorrow?   _____

6. How many pieces of pepperoni are left?   _____

Answers on page 190.

World City Nicknames

Each clue below describes a world city. Use the city names in the box to help you fill in the crossword.

Bangkok	Calgary	Manila	Prague
Bombay	Florence	Montreal	Rome
Budapest	London	Paris	Venice

ACROSS

3. The Square Mile
6. City of a Hundred Spires
7. Pearl of the Danube
9. The Stampede City
10. City of Lilies

DOWN

1. Pearl of the Orient
2. Bollywood
4. City of Saints
5. Bride of the Sea
6. City of Lights

7. Venice of the East
8. The Eternal City

Answers on page 190.

Hung Out to Dry

To find the message hidden in this laundry, start at the top left with the first letter, **I**, and then write down every third letter (starting with **F** onward). Cross out each letter as you use it. Next, start at the top again, and write down the second letter from the beginning, then every second letter, but don't count the letters you've already crossed out. Finally, go to the top one last time and write (in order) every letter that remains. Divide the letters into words, but don't change their order. If you do it correctly, you'll find the answer to this riddle: What advice does Mom have for people whose clothes seem to stay wet forever?

Answer: _____

_____ !

Answer on page 190.

Silly Signs

Can you spot the mistakes in the signs? Each sign has a word that needs to be replaced by its homonym.

(**Homonyms** are words that sound the same but are spelled differently.) Cross out the mistakes, and then write the correct word on the lines.

Pay fair at tollbooth.

No Eating Aloud!

One Our Parking

1. _____ 2. _____ 3. _____

Dear Crossing

No Parking Hear

Deposit male in slot.

4. _____ 5. _____ 6. _____

If elevator is broken, take the stares.

Please throw waist in the trash can.

No Threw Traffic

7. _____ 8. _____ 9. _____

Answers on page 190.

Phone Fun!

Grab your calculator, and try this math puzzle on for size. Then share it with your friends!

1. Write down the first 3 digits of your phone number. (do NOT include the area code) _____

2. Multiply by 80 _____

3. Add 1 _____

4. Multiply by 250 _____

5. Add the last 4 digits of your phone number _____

6. Add the last 4 digits of your phone number again _____

7. Subtract 250 _____

8. Divide by 2 _____

What is the result? _____

Answer on page 190.

You've Got Mail

Each answer in this puzzle is a 4-letter word made by putting 2 U.S. postal abbreviations together. For example, MA (Massachusetts) + IL (Illinois) make MAIL. To help, we've given definitions for the answers as well as a list of all the state abbreviations you'll need. **Note:** No state abbreviation are used more than once and not all are used.

State Abbreviations

AK AL AR AZ CA CO CT DE FL GA HI IA ID IL
IN KS KY LA MA ME MI MN MO MS MT NC ND NE
NH NJ NM NV NY OH OR PA RI SC SD TN VA WA

1. Striped candy object on a Christmas tree   _____

2. Tag or hide-and-seek   _____

3. Boats such as Noah's in the Bible   _____

4. Thing to hold sand in at the beach   _____

5. Barely go into the water at the beach   _____

6. Penny or dime, for example   _____

7. More than several   _____

8. Top edges of coffee cups   _____

9. Hot stuff from a volcano   _____

10. Do you _____ if I change the channel?   _____

Answers on page 190.

Five Brothers

The Baker family has 5 boys. The boys are lined up from the shortest to the tallest. Read the clues to figure out each boy's name.

A.   B.   C.   D.   E.

Patrick is taller than Sam.

Brent is taller than Martin.

Martin is taller than Jason.

Sam is taller than Brent.

Write the name of each boy beside his matching letter.

A. _____

B. _____

C. _____

D. _____

E. _____

Answers on page 190.

Get Ready to Recycle

Recycling is reusing something to make something else. In this puzzle you will "recycle" the maze by ending next to where you started.

Answer on page 191.

Counting the Days

Freddy, Felicia, Phil, and Phyllis like to "collect" days of the year. Freddy likes all the days in April that start or end with a 2. Felicia likes all the days in May, June, and July that start or end with a 3. Phil likes all the days in August that start or end with a 1. And Phyllis likes all the days in September, October, November, and December that end with a 4. Based on those numbers, can you figure out which friend has the biggest collection of days?

Freddy: _____

Felicia: _____

Phil: _____

Phyllis: _____

Answers on page 191.

Math Palindromes

A **palindrome** is a word, phrase, or sentence that reads the same both backward and forward. For example, **MOM** and **DAD** are palindromes. A math palindrome is a number that has the same value when read either backward or forward, such as 141 or 76,367. Solve the problems, then put the answers in the numbered spaces on the grid.

ACROSS

1. Arabian Nights or 1 more than the number of years in a millennium

5. 3 times 1-Across

6. 165 less than the number of feet in a mile

8. 5,933 times 4

10. 97,368 divided by 2

11. (23 times 23) plus (6 times 6)

12. 11-Across plus 14-Down

14. New York City telephone area code or 10 less than 14-Down

15. 10,737,016 short of 500 million

DOWN

1. The year before Bill Clinton was first elected U.S. president

2. Dalmatians or 1 more than the number of years in a century

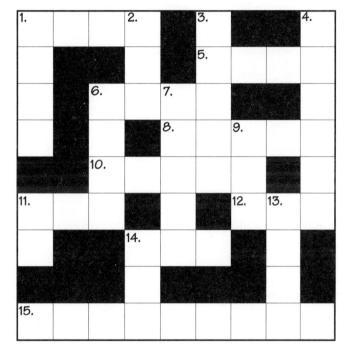

3. 5-Across plus 8-Across plus 10-Across plus 13-Down plus half of 14-Down

4. 732,238 minus 1

6. 27,225 divided by 5

7. (14-Across times 11-Down) plus 9-Down plus 14-Across plus 2

9. Another type of airplane, or 40 short of 12-Across

11. The speed limit on many U.S. highways or the number of U.S. states plus the number of fingers on 1 hand

13. 8 times 1-Across

14. A certain digit repeated 3 times

Answers on page 191.

A Trip Across America

Start at Olympia, and keep traveling from city to city until you reach Tallahassee. Just be sure you only pass through capital cities to complete your journey!

Start

Olympia	Salem	Boise	Cheyenne	Pierre	Helena	Bismarck
Dallas	San Francisco	Portland	Seattle	Flagstaff	Vancouver	Sacramento
Des Moines	Carson City	Santa Fe	Salt Lake City	Denver	Phoenix	Juneau
Topeka	Laramie	Anchorage	Houston	Las Vegas	Boulder	Pittsburgh
Oklahoma	Detroit	Memphis	Louisville	Kokomo	Chicago	Twin Falls
Austin	St. Louis	Roswell	Birmingham	Spokane	Ogden	Oshkosh
St. Paul	Kansas City	Boston	Albany	Trenton	Harrisburg	Providence
Madison	Fairbanks	Annapolis	Hilo	Orlando	Dodge City	Concord
Little Rock	Newark	Augusta	Rock Hill	Raleigh	Columbus	Montpelier
Springfield	Atlantic City	Dover	Los Angeles	Columbia	Tampa	Butte
Indianapolis	Tulsa	Lincoln	Tucson	Nashville	Waterloo	Cleveland
Baton Rouge	New Orleans	Jefferson City	Idaho Falls	Richmond	Frankfort	Hartford
Montgomery	Tupelo	Jackson	Charlotte	Dayton	Palm Springs	Atlanta
Honolulu	Charleston	Lansing	Sioux City	Minneapolis	Miami	Tallahassee

Finish

Answer on page 191.

Worldwide Scramble

All of the scrambled words below are the names of foreign countries. Rearrange the letters to discover what they are.

1. LAITY _____

2. AAASUTRIL _____

3. RGUHANY _____

4. NACDAA _____

5. DALECIN _____

6. AIHNC _____

7. REYKUT _____

8. BALRIZ _____

9. NAMEGRY _____

10. COXIME _____

Answers on page 191.

Number Crossword

ACROSS

1. The number right before 1,000

4. 3-Down minus 44-Across

6. 42-Down written backward

8. 1,696 times 4

10. The number right after 340

12. The last two digits of 30-Across

13. 28-Across plus 15-Down

14. 3 more than 150

16. 41-Across plus 29-Across

18. 5 more than 400

19. 34-Down plus 26-Across

20. 11-Down plus 32-Across

22. 1-Down minus 26-Across

23. 3 times 6

25. 18-Across plus 3-Down

26. 115 plus itself

27. 26-Down minus 42-Down

28. The number right after 30

29. 1-Across divided by 9

30. 20-Across plus 45-Across

31. 19-Across plus 26-Down

32. 1-Across minus 17-Down

33. 33-Down plus 1-Down

35. 12 more than 10-Across

36. The last two digits of 22-Across

38. 42-Down plus 44-Across

39. 27-Down written backward

41. 29-Down written backward

43. The last two digits of 19-Across

44. 14 plus 9

45. 29-Across times 3

DOWN

1. 242 times 4

2. 1-Across minus 44-Across

3. 49 plus itself

4. 25-Across plus 26-Across

5. 28-Across plus 44-Across

6. 10 more than 10-Across

7. 2 more than 700

9. 30-Down plus 1-Down

11. 1-Across times 2

15. 5 more than half of 100

17. The first two digits of 24-Down

18. 44-Across plus 19-Across

19. 18-Across minus 4-Across

20. 204 plus 49

21. 1-Across minus 3-Down

22. 10-Across plus 19-Across

23. 43-Across plus 15-Down

24. 400 doubled

26. 13 more than 200

27. 23-Across plus 29-Across

29. 1-Across plus 17-Down

30. 3,413 minus 274

31. 40-Down times 3

32. 40-Down plus 42-Down

33. The first three digits of 11-Down

34. 17-Down times 2

35. 34-Down plus 14-Across

36. 26-Across plus 42-Down

37. 4-Down plus 17-Down

40. 11 plus itself

42. Two less than three quarters of 100

Answers on page 191.

Under Pressure

You have exactly 15 minutes to answer the following questions. Have a pencil with an eraser handy, and get a clock or watch to time yourself. When the 15 minutes are up, put your pencil down and stop whether you're finished or not. Ready to start? Go!

If a spider has 6 legs, write the number 8 in the blank. If it has 8 legs, write the number 6. _____ Take the word SHRUB, cross out the **R,** rearrange the letters to get another plant, and write that plant's name in the blank. _____ If your answer is the last name of a U.S. president in the 21st century, cross out the answer and put a **W** in the blank instead. If the earth revolves around the Sun, leave the next blank empty. If the Sun revolves around the earth, fill in the blank with the words I GOOFED! _____

Count the number of words in this sentence that begin with a consonant, and write that number in the blank. _____ If Groundhog Day comes later in February than Valentine's Day, write a **G** in the blank. If Valentine's Day comes later, write a **V** in the blank. _____

Circle the phrase that doesn't belong here: CLUB SANDWICH, DIAMOND MERCHANT, HEART ASSOCIATION, QUEEN ELIZABETH.
Whichever letter appears the most in your circled answer, write that letter in this blank. _____ Put your pencil down. Now put your right hand on your left elbow, and put your left hand on your right elbow. In that position, lift both arms straight up, put them gently behind your head, lean back in your chair, take a deep breath, and relax. Aaaaah! Doesn't that feel good? OK, go back and pick up your pencil. If you've filled in any blank with a **W,** cross it out, and put in a **T.** If you've written 15 in any blank, cross it out, and write in the 15th letter of the alphabet. Fill in any empty blanks with an **S.** If you've filled in a blank with a 6, cross it out, and put in an **I.** Now read all the letters in the blanks in order from top to bottom, and write them at the bottom of this page. Now take the **R** that you took from SHRUB and put it at the end of those letters. Put an apostrophe after the **T.** Put a space after the **S.** That leads to a two-word message that should make you very happy. If you got the correct message, congratulations! You do know how to think under pressure.

Answer on page 191.

P Is for Preboarding

How many things can you find that start with the letter **P?** Finding 40 would be Pretty darn good. Finding 45 or more would be almost Perfect!

Answers on page 192.

169

Presidential Trivia

Solve the clues below with the last names of U.S. presidents, and write the answer in the boxes on the next page. When you've finished, read the shaded boxes from top to bottom to find the answer to this trivia question: Who was the 34th president and in office when Alaska entered the Union?

1. His home was called Monticello.

2. He was born William Jefferson Blythe IV.

3. He was the first president to appear on television.

4. In 1886, he became the only president to be married in the White House.

5. This president was the tallest president at 6′4″.

6. The other father-and-son presidential duo, after John Adams and John Quincy Adams.

7. He was the only president to serve who was not elected either president or vice president.

8. He was the only president to have a U.S. state named after him.

9. He was the youngest elected president.

10. This president appeared in 53 films.

1. ☐ ☐ ☐ ☐ ☐ ☐ ☐ ☐ ☐

2. ☐ ☐ ☐ ☐ ☐ ☐ ☐

3. ☐ ☐ ☐ ☐ ☐ ☐ ☐ ☐ ☐

4. ☐ ☐ ☐ ☐ ☐ ☐ ☐ ☐ ☐

5. ☐ ☐ ☐ ☐ ☐ ☐ ☐

6. ☐ ☐ ☐ ☐

7. ☐ ☐ ☐ ☐

8. ☐ ☐ ☐ ☐ ☐ ☐ ☐ ☐ ☐ ☐

9. ☐ ☐ ☐ ☐ ☐ ☐ ☐

10. ☐ ☐ ☐ ☐ ☐ ☐

Answer: _____

Answers on page 192.

Super Crossword

ACROSS

1. Tokyo is its capital

6. Goes by airplane

11. Stadium

12. Soup scoop

13. Start

14. Stopped sleeping

15. Pop a question

17. Remain

21. "___ ___ ___ ___   ___ ___!" (what to say when you're in big trouble): 2 words

26. You watch shows on them

28. Summer or winter

29. Run at an easy pace

30. Yards needed for a first down

32. Atmospheric layer that's in trouble

36. Creative thoughts

41. Person who uses oars

42. Australian "bear"

43. Lightning appears in this form

44. Wading bird with long legs

DOWN

1. Poke

2. "___ ___ ___ we there yet?"

3. Thing to hang your hat on

4. "I'd like to buy ___ ___ ___" (on "Wheel of Fortune"): 2 words

5. Grandmother

6. Frosted (cereal)

7. Legal rule

8. "What can ___   ___ ___ for you?": 2 words

9. Animal like a moose

10. Use your eyes

16. What the sun does on a sunny day

17. City crossings: Abbreviation

18. A football is placed on it for the kickoff

19. Abbreviation for a state next to Mississippi

20. "Sure!"

22. Got a match going

23. "___ ___ ___ favor" ("please" in Spanish)

24. Letters on a 6 on a telephone

25. Ending for "great" or "small"

27. Election participants

31. Popular sneakers brand

32. Sphere

33. Place to visit animals

34. Hedwig in Harry Potter books

35. Basketball hoop strings

37. Poodle or collie

38. It's on the side of your face

39. Ginger ___ ___ ___ (soft drink)

40. Used a chair

1.	2.	3.	4.	5.		6.	7.	8.	9.	10.
11.						12.				
13.						14.				
				15.	16.					
17.	18.	19.	20.		21.		22.	23.	24.	25.
26.				27.						
28.							29.			
				30.		31.				
32.	33.	34.	35.			36.	37.	38.	39.	40.
41.						42.				
43.						44.				

Answers on page 192.

Spouting Off

Copy each picture piece into the correct numbered spot on the grid on the following page. When you're finished, you'll have a complete picture!

	1	2	3	4
A				
B				
C				
D				

Answers on page 192.

Carnival Rebus

A rebus is a riddle that uses pictures and letters instead of words. Can you figure out these objects that you'd find at a carnival?

 + K +

_____

_____

_____

F +  + S

_____

PR +  + S

_____

 + 10 + D

_____

Answers on page 192.

ANSWERS

Letter T Match (page 6)

Tepee
Tree
Truck
Tiger
Triangle
Tricycle

Word Play (page 7)

multiply; above; rough; young; loosen; absent; narrow; difficult
Answer: Maryland (merry land)

Choose Wisely! (page 8)

1. hard; 2. car; 3. dolls; 4. milk; 5. roses; 6. meat; 7. flute; 8. pals; 9. bees; 10. fast

What Not to Wear? (page 9)

flip-flops, dress (not cold-weather clothes)

A Fruity Puzzle (page 10)

1. apple; 2. lemon; 3. orange; 4. grapes; 5. peach; 6. cherry; 7. strawberry; 8. watermelon

What's Your Number? (page 11)

F I V E
O
U   S I X
T H R E E
W   V
O N E   E
    I   N I N E
    G
    H
    T E N

What's at the Theater? (page 12)

1. movie; 2. popcorn; 3. soda; 4. tickets; 5. candy

Number Crossword (page 13)

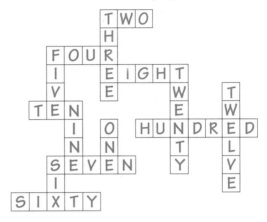

A Different Order (page 14)

mope=poem; peas=apes; free=reef; bear=bare; coin=icon; scat=cats; tuna=aunt; evil= live; rate=tear; salt=last

Frame-Up (page 15)

L I B R A R Y E A
E   R
G   T
A   I
B   S
A   T
L   O
L   P
E S A R E V E N E

Pen It In (page 16)

1. open; 2. spend; 3. pencil; 4. penny; 5. penguin

Works of Art (page 17)

1. tray; 2. star; 3. train; 4. heart; 5. Earth; 6. feather; 7. triangle

Answers

Flower Fun (page 18)

Middle Management (page 19)

ask; jam; any; odd; own; fix; icy; why
Answer: sandwich

Picture Crossword (page 20)

State Lines (page 21)

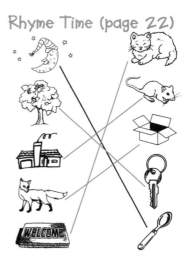

The other state is Louisiana.

Rhyme Time (page 22)

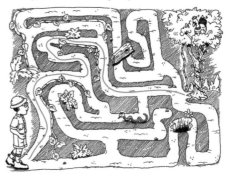

Sweet Spot (page 23)

So they can have sweet dreams!

Jungle Maze (page 24)

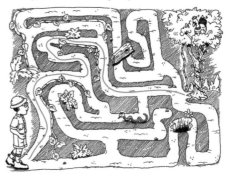

Sheepish Riddle (page 25)

1. watch; 2. bike; 3. shark; 4. shell; 5. shoe;
6. shovel; 7. shapes; 8. brush; 9. ship; 10. shadow
Answer: At the baa baa shop

C-Ya (page 26)

1. face; 2. sun; 3. corn; 4. book; 5. church;
6. clock; 7. chicken

In Outer Space (page 28)

1. sun; 2. planet; 3. star; 4. comet; 5. meteor;
6. spacecraft; 7. orbit; 8. moon

Tiny Creatures (page 29)
1. ant; 2. bee; 3. fly; 4. moth; 5. snail; 6. wasp

Gigantic Creatures (page 29)
1. python; 2. crocodile; 3. hippopotamus;
4. rhinoceros; 5. giraffe; 6. elephant

'Tis the Season (page 30)
1. winter; 2. puddle; 3. snow; 4. lightning; 5. fog;
6. storm; 7. summer; 8. wind; 9. thunder;
10. autumn
Answer: Springtime!

Picture Word Search (page 31)

What Am I? (page 32)
A parade

M Is for Many States (page 33)
Maine (6); Maryland (8); Massachusetts (7);
Michigan (3); Minnesota (2); Mississippi (5);
Missouri (4); Montana (1)

Star Search (page 34)
You will be a success in solving this puzzle!

Picture Crossword (page 35)

P	I	Z	Z	A			D	R	U	M	S
E				R			E				C
A			R	I	N	G	S				A
R				O			K				L
S	T	R	A	W			S	T	O	V	E

Wild Cats (page 36)

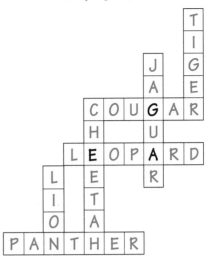

Cross It Out (page 37)
Answer: your age

Weather or Not (page 38)
1. shirt; 2. hippo; 3. orange; 4. vest; 5. ear;
6. lamp
Answer: shovel

Front and Back (page 39)

E	R	R	O	R	O	U	G	H
T								Y
U								E
L								N
F								A
R								C
A								O
W								R
D	L	E	I	Y	S	I	O	N

Charlie's Painting (page 40)
Charlie painted the picture of a leaf.

Answers

Beginnings and Endings (page 41)
1. mom; 2. roar; 3. willow; 4. knock; 5. success;
6. peep; 7. erase; 8. rooster; 9. window; 10. kick;
11. noun

Dyeing to Be Found (page 42)
1. canary; 2. hazel; 3. pink; 4. aqua; 5. ruby;
6. yellow; 7. purple; 8. silver; 9. peach; 10. rose;
11. green; 12. black; 13. pumpkin; 14. red;
15. white

Don't Miss the Bus (page 44)
1. three; 2. stars; 3. the third row; 4. birdbath
with birds in it; 5. QT; 6. behind his head;
7. mail carrier; 8. Math 5; 9. apple; 10. none

Dollars and Cents (page 45)

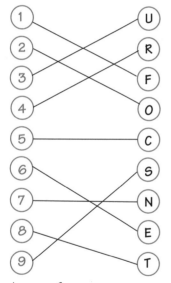

Answer: four cents

Filling Good (page 46)

Hidden message: The answer is jellyfish.

Doing Their Jobs (page 47)
Barber=scissors; Librarian=books; Dog
walker=leash; Football player=helmet; Janitor=
mop; Dentist=toothbrush; Photographer=
camera; Mail carrier=letters; Cook=pots and
pans; Basketball referee=whistle; Weather-
person=map; Santa Claus=bag of toys

Forward and Back (page 48)

Magic Letters (page 49)
1. bat, rat; 2. hoof, roof; 3. pen, pin; 4. honey,
money; 5. cart, dart

Picture This (page 50)

Fly Away Home (page 51)

The monarch butterfly migrates south for the winter, just as many birds do.

Let It BE (page 52)

1. bee; 2. bell; 3. best; 4. berry; 5. behave;
6. bedroom; 7. beginning; 8. because; 9. beautiful

Picture Crossword (page 53)

F	O	R	K				
O			I		S	W	A	N
U		T	A	N	K		E
R	O	P	E		I		C
					S	O	C	K

Round Up (page 54)

1. beetle; 2. cricket; 3. hornet; 4. cockroach;
5. butterfly; 6. mosquito; 7. grasshopper;
8. dragonfly

Subtract or Add (page 55)

Answer: a nervous wreck!

Synonym Unscramble (page 56)

1. upset; 2. cruel; 3. chuckle; 4. beautiful;
5. photo; 6. trip; 7. interesting; 8. sport; 9. scary;
10. suitcase; 11. doctor; 12. draw

Egg-cellent! (page 57)

Weather Compounds (page 58)

1. rainbow; 2. sunlight; 3. snowflakes;
4. cloudburst; 5. whirlwind; 6. hailstone

Tricky Triangles (page 59)

1. 5; 2. 7; 3. 13; 4. 13

Triplets (page 60)

1. carpets; 2. mushrooms

Cool Codes (page 61)

I scream. You scream. We all scream for ice cream!

Animal Actions (page 62)

Answers

Farmer Pete's Riddle (page 63)

☐ =p; △ =o; ◯ =c; ⬡ =r; ◇ =n

Answer: I want popcorn!

Name That Homonym (page 64)

1. two; 2. bear; 3. there; 4. meat; 5. hair; 6. hear;
7. flour; 8. boar

Brain Food (page 65)

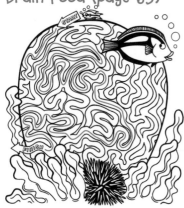

Wacky Wordies (page 66)

1. giant panda; 2. high tide; 3. quarterback;
4. get out; 5. fill in the blanks; 6. no right turn

What Comes Before? (page 67)

Question: What do you call a song about cars?
Answer: A car-tune!

Fishy Squares (page 68)

1. 7; 2. 11; 3. 15

Letters in Colors A (page 69)

green

Letters in Colors B (page 69)

yellow

Crazy Circles (page 70)

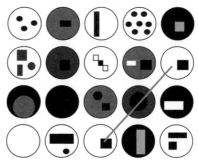

Take Note (page 71)

Answer: To pick up some rapping paper.

A Cagey Riddle (page 72)

1. impossible; 2. hawk; 3. alive; 4. vanish; 5. elect;
6. yesterday; 7. odor; 8. unique; 9. castle;
10. observe; 11. veil; 12. empty; 13. roots;
14. evil; 15. drag
Answer: I have you covered!

Baker Bob's Puzzling Pies (page 73)
(other answers are possible)

1.
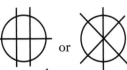 or

2.

3.

4.

Half-Word Puzzle (page 74)

By the Numbers (page 75)
1. seven; 2. three; 3. ten; 4. nine; 5. one; 6. eight;
7. six; 8. five; 9. two; 10. four

Take Me to Your Mummy (page 76)

Missing Shapes (page 77)

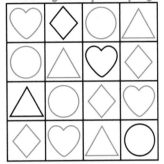

What Am I? (page 78)
Answer: a comb

Bottles, Bottles Everywhere (page 80)

Call a Doctor (page 81)
1. medicine; 2. physician; 3. hospital; 4. disease;
5. nurse; 6. bandage; 7. needle

Fun with Leftover Letters (page 82)
Answer: a flip flop

Look for These C's (page 83)
1. cactus; 2. calendar; 3. camel; 4. candles;
5. candy; 6. car; 7. carrot; 8. castle; 9. cat;
10. caterpillar; 11. cheese; 12. cherry; 13. chicks;
14. chip; 15. chocolate; 16. circle; 17. city;
18. clock; 19. cloud; 20. coin; 21. cookie;
22. corn; 23. cow; 24. cowboy; 25. crayon
(other answers are possible)

Answers

Tricky 2's (page 84)

$2 \times 2 \times 2 + 2 \div 2 = 5$

Magic Square (page 84)

10	15	8	33
9	11	13	33
14	7	12	33
33	33	33	33

Are You Packed Yet? (page 85)

Black and White All Over (page 87)

Heartbreaker Challenge (page 88)

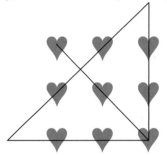

Lend Me an Ear (page 89)

1. bear; 2. heard; 3. tears; 4. pearl; 5. beard;
6. early; 7. hearts; 8. nearest; 9. fearful;
10. learning; 11. unclear; 12. nuclear;
13. Goodyear; 14. spearmint; 15. disappear

Spell It Out (page 90)

frog, cake, plane, ax, home, goat, ham, dart
State: Oklahoma

Mega Matchup (page 91)

A-6 and D-2; C-4 and E-1; B-1 and E-5

At the Park (page 92)

1. tree; 2. grass; 3. swing; 4. slide; 5. bench;
6. path; 7. duck; 8. pond; 9. kite; 10. flower

Sum-mertime (page 93)

Answer: So, did you have sum fun?

Going in Circles (page 94)

1. clock; 2. top; 3. watch; 4. wheel; 5. planet;
6. track; 7. carousel; 8. electron

Make-a-Word (page 95)

1. amputate; 2. cabinet; 3. cannonball; 4. capital;
5. catalog; 6. doormat; 7. heartache; 8. informed;
9. meadow; 10. noontime; 11. redhead;
12. together

W Is for Watching and Waiting (page 96)

1. wader; 2. waiter; 3. wall; 4. walrus; 5. wand;
6. wart; 7. wash; 8. washer; 9. watch; 10. water;
11. waterfall; 12. watermelon; 13. wax; 14. webs;
15. weight-lifter; 16. weights; 17. whale; 18. wheel;
19. wick; 20. wig; 21. window; 22. wings;
23. witch; 24. wizard; 25. wolf; 26. woman;
27. woods; 28. worm; 29. wreath
(other answers are possible)

Kitchen Mix-Up (page 97)

1. pot; 2. pan; 3. bowl; 4. mug; 5. stove; 6. sink;
7. table; 8. spoon; 9. plate; 10. towel

Road Sign Shapes (page 98)

1. Stop; 2. Yield; 3. One Way; 4. Do Not Enter;
5. Railroad Crossing; 6. Interstate Route; 7. U.S.
Route; 8. State Route

Area Code (page 99)

Answer: Cell phone users who talk loudly in
public without regard for others are being cell-
fish! (selfish)

Anthony's Ant Words (page 100)

1. plant; 2. pants; 3. giant; 4. antlers; 5. want;
6. slant; 7. grant; 8. panther; 9. antenna;
10. tantrum

Race Through Space (page 101)

2 Times 2 (page 102)

1. George; 2. Miami; 3. decide; 4. photograph;
5. escapes; 6. straightest

Rest Stop (page 103)

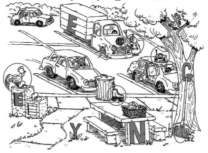

Answer: energy

Know Your Numbers (page 104)

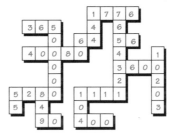

Similar Sounds (page 105)

1. ate, eight; 2. won, one; 3. know, no; 4. meet,
meat; 5. I, eye; 6. way, weigh; 7. blew, blue; 8. sail,
sale; 9. Knights, nights; 10. fare, fair; 11. read,
Red; 12. guessed, guest; 13. hose, hoes; 14. sent,
cent, scent; 15. seas, seize, sees

1 Word+1 Word=1 Word (page 106)

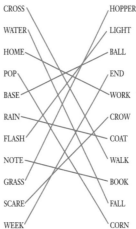

CROSS   HOPPER
WATER   LIGHT
HOME   BALL
POP   END
BASE   WORK
RAIN   CROW
FLASH   COAT
NOTE   WALK
GRASS   BOOK
SCARE   FALL
WEEK   CORN

Answers

3-Letter Challenge (page 107)
1. coyote; 2. gorilla; 3. leopard; 4. elephant

Inside the Opposites (page 108)
1. puppy; 2. goose; 3. pillow; 4. spout; 5. closet;
6. hotel; 7. swell; 8. fasten; 9. topple; 10. shrink;
11. enrich; 12. saddle; 13. bold; 14. delight;
15. thunder

Basketball Signs (page 109)
1. Start the clock; 2. Stop the clock; 3. Traveling;
4. Technical foul; 5. Score

Pairs to Compare (page 110)
1. thermometer; 2. hat; 3. sled; 4. swimming;
5. floor; 6. taste; 7. water; 8. glove; 9. eleventh;
10. boat; 11. down; 12. vegetable

Avalanche Maze (page 111)

Number Facts (page 112)
1. 12 Inches in a Foot
2. 365 Days in a Year
3. 24 Hours in a Day
4. 3 Wheels on a Tricycle
5. 52 Weeks in a Year
6. 100 Centimeters in a Meter
7. 4 Quarts in a Gallon
8. 16 Ounces in a Pound
9. 60 Minutes in an Hour
10. 10 Years in a Decade
11. 26 Letters of the Alphabet
12. 8 Tentacles on an Octopus
13. 4 Quarters in a Dollar
14. 60 Seconds in a Minute
15. 100 Years in a Century
16. 50 Stars on the U.S. Flag

What's Wrong in Time? (page 113)
1. basketball court; 2. car; 3. flying disc; 4. inline
skates; 5. laptop computer; 6. mountain bike;
7. pay phone; 8. stop sign; 9. streetlight;
10. televisions

PANdemonium (page 114)
1. pancakes; 2. panda; 3. pansy; 4. pantry;
5. Panama; 6. panther; 7. pants; 8. panic

Eagle Eyes (page 115)
A farmer

Christmas Clues (page 116)
1. Frosty; 2. carols; 3. Rudolph; 4. presents;
5. ornaments; 6. Bah; 7. white; 8. Santa; 9. angel
Answer: frostbite

Country Balloons (page 117)
1. Peru, U; 2. Kenya, A; 3. India, I; 4. Japan, A;
5. Egypt, T; 6. Spain, S; 7. Korea, A; 8. Brazil, R;
9. England, L. Answer: Australia

OR Bits (page 118)

State Match (page 119)
A. Wisconsin; B. New York; C. Texas; D. Idaho;
E. Montana; F. Florida

Spell It Out (page 120)
Portugal

Anatonyms Challenge (page 121)
1. face; 2. foot; 3. eye; 4. shoulder; 5. arm;
6. finger; 7. nose; 8. elbow; 9. skin; 10. mouth

Geography Quiz (page 122)
1. Asia, Australia, Europe, Antarctica, South
   America, North America, Africa. Largest: Asia
2. Erie, Michigan, Superior, Ontario, Huron.
   Biggest: Superior
3. George Washington, Thomas Jefferson,
   Theodore Roosevelt, Abraham Lincoln. In
   common: They were all presidents.
4. Alaska, Hawaii
5. Mt. McKinley, Alaska; Death Valley, California
Bonus: Four Corners Monument is in Colorado,
   Utah, Arizona, and New Mexico.

Missing Shapes (page 123)

Sentence Riddles (page 124)
1. singing in the rain; 2. circles under the eyes;
3. think outside the box; 4. underwater; 5. jack-in-
the-box; 6. flat tire; 7. long face; 8. horsing around

The Professor's Lists (page 125)
A. one thousand; B. 55

Restaurant Scene (page 126)
(other answers are possible)
1. Things that are wrong: giant toadstool at the
   counter; tire under the counter; hammer on the
   counter with the salt and pepper shakers;
   clothes iron in a booth; treasure chest.
2. These start with **C**: candle, cash register, clock,
   coffee, coffeemaker, coffeepot, counter, cup
3. H-U-N-G-R-Y

Mystery Animals (page 127)
1. hippopotamus; 2. lion; 3. camel; 4. aardvark;
5. orangutan; 6. armadillo; 7. beluga whale;
8. spider; 9. raccoon; 10. duck

Once Around the Big Block (page 128)

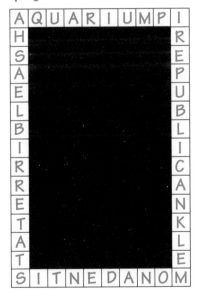

What in the World? (page 129)
1. New Year's Day; 2. Easter; 3. Labor Day;
4. Christmas; 5. Halloween; 6. Memorial Day;
7. Presidents' Day; 8. Valentine's Day; 9. Mother's
Day; 10. Father's Day; 11. Thanksgiving;
12. Earth Day; 13. St. Patrick's Day; 14. Fourth of
July
Message: Welcome to Earth!

Answers

What a Mess! (page 130)

Number Patterns (page 131)

1. 56, 67, 78 (Numbers increase by 11 each time.)
2. 21, 28, 36 (Add 1, add 2, add 3, add 4, and so on.)
3. 64, 73, 82 (Numbers increase by 9 each time.)
4. 17, 16, 21 (Add 5 to the first number, and subtract 1 from the next number.)
5. 5, 25, 6 (A number is followed by its square.)
6. 21, 34, 55 (Each number is added to the number before it.)
7. One digit is twice the other digit; the numbers are divisible by 3.
8. The 2 outer digits add up to the middle digit.
9. The middle digit is half the sum of the outer digits.

International Signs (page 132)

1. Lost & found; 2. Currency exchange; 3. Falling rocks; 4. Drinking water; 5. No entry; 6. Gift shop; 7. Information; 8. Viewing area; 9. Customs; 10. Hiking trail

Fun with Opposites (page 133)

1. shortstop; 2. farmer; 3. soldier; 4. offering; 5. plastic; 6. ostrich; 7. laundry; 8. flower; 9. closer; 10. chocolate; 11. orchard; 12. positive

Farmer Green's Veggies (page 134)

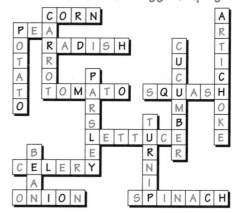

Beam in on B's (page 135)

1. baby; 2. backpack; 3. bag; 4. ballerina; 5. balloon; 6. banana; 7. bandana; 8. baseball; 9. basket; 10. bat; 11. bear; 12. beard; 13. bell; 14. belt; 15. bench; 16. beret; 17. bicycle; 18. bird; 19. blanket; 20. blimp; 21. boat; 22. bone; 23. book; 24. boomerang; 25. boots; 26. bottle; 27. bowling ball; 28. braids; 29. bow tie; 30. box; 31. boxer; 32. brain; 33. branch; 34. bread; 35. bricks; 36. broom; 37. brush; 38. bucket; 39. bug; 40. buildings; 41. bull; 42. bus; 43. bush; 44. butterfly
(other answers are possible)

Where Do They Live? (page 136)

Answer: pen pals

Follow the Arrows (page 137)

188

Word Morphs (page 138)
HARD, card, care, case, ease, EASY
DUCK, deck, peck, peak, beak, bean, beat, seat, swat, SWAN

Plus or Minus (page 139)
1. $7+2-5=4$,
2. $5-4+8=9$,
3. $1+3-1=3$,
4. $2+4+6=12$,
5. $9+1-2=8$,
6. $8-6+7+1=10$,
7. $3-1+4+5=11$,
8. $4+6-1-2=7$,
9. $6+5-7+1=5$,
10. $9-4+2-3=4$

Splish Splash (page 140)

Terrible 2's (page 141)
Tookey: 38; Toomey: 10

Anagram Detective (page 142)
1. dormitory, dirty room; 2. schoolmaster, the classroom; 3. Elvis, lives; 4. silent, listen; 5. public art galleries, large picture halls, I bet; 6. the detectives, detect thieves; 7. eleven plus two, twelve plus one; 8. a gentleman, elegant man; 9. a decimal point, I'm a dot in place; 10. vacation times, I'm not as active

Now What? (page 143)
1. 2. 3.
4. 5. 6.

Word Trios (page 144)
1. blue, red, yellow; 2. plane, train, car; 3. ship, boat, ferry; 4. whale, fish, crab; 5. tree, bush, grass; 6. pear, plum, grape; 7. coat, hat, sweater; 8. doll, ball, top; 9. hammer, saw, drill; 10. chair, bench, stool; 11. shoe, boot, slipper; 12. river, lake, sea

Box by Box (page 145)
1: B. Parachute school
2: A. To make up for a bad summer
3: C. A plane that makes short hops

I Love a Parade! (page 146)

Math Mystery (page 147)
The answer is your original number from step 1.

Surroundings (page 148)
1. crossword; 2. landmark; 3. patient; 4. pleasure; 5. foolish; 6. lipstick; 7. miserable; 8. peculiar; 9. peppermint; 10. platinum; 11. deliver; 12. decimal; 13. locomotive; 14. textile

Answers

Word Bingo (page 149)
roller coaster, police station or officer, free space, tennis court, bookstore

Pen Pal Letters (page 150)
1. OK, Oklahoma; 2. HI, Hawaii; 3. OR, Oregon;
4. OH, Ohio; 5. IN, Indiana; 6. AL, Alabama;
7. MT, Montana; 8. WA, Washington; 9. MS, Mississippi

Check This Out! (page 151)

Barbershop Bloopers (page 152)

Squish—Squash (page 153)
1. rose, iris; 2. lily, daisy; 3. tulip, lilac; 4. pansy, poppy; 5. violet, orchid; 6. begonia, petunia;
7. marigold, daffodil; 8. geranium, gardenia;
9. sunflower, buttercup; 10. carnation, dandelion

Pizza Delivery (page 154)
1. Patty: 1 from A, 1 from B, 1 from C
2. Phil: 1 from A, 2 from B
3. Pablo: 6 from C
4. Pete: 2 from A, 1 from B
5. 3 pizza slices leftover, 2 from B, 1 from C
6. Pieces of pepperoni left: 10

World City Nicknames (page 155)

Hung Out to Dry (page 156)
Answer: If at first you don't succeed, dry, dry again!

Silly Signs (page 157)
1. fare; 2. allowed; 3. hour; 4. deer; 5. here;
6. mail; 7. stairs; 8. waste; 9. through

Phone Fun! (page 158)
The answer is your phone number!

You've Got Mail (page 159)
1. cane; 2. game; 3. arks; 4. pail; 5. wade; 6. coin;
7. many; 8. rims; 9. lava; 10. mind

Five Brothers (page 160)
A. Jason; B. Martin; C. Brent; D. Sam;
E. Patrick

Get Ready to Recycle (page 161)

Counting the Days (page 162)

Freddy: 12 days (April 2, 12, 20, 21, 22, 23, 24, 25, 26, 27, 28, 29)

Felicia (the winner): 14 days (May 3, 13, 23, 30, 31; June 3, 13, 23, 30; July 3, 13, 23, 30, 31)

Phil: 13 days (August 1, 10, 11, 12, 13, 14, 15, 16, 17, 18, 19, 21, 31)

Phyllis: 12 days (September 4, 14, 24; October 4, 14, 24; November 4, 14, 24; December 4, 14, 24)

Math Palindromes (page 163)

1	0	0	1	■	8	■	7
9	■	0	■	3	0	0	3
9	■	5	1	1	5	■	2
1	■	4	■	2	3	7	3	2
■	■	4	8	6	8	4	■	3
5	6	5	■	2	■	7	8	7
5	■	■	2	1	2	■	0
■	■	2	■	■	2	■	0
4	8	9	2	6	2	9	8	4

A Trip Across America (page 164)

Start

Olympia	Salem	Boise	Cheyenne	Pierre	Helena	Bismarck
Dallas	San Francisco	Portland	Seattle	Flagstaff	Vancouver	Sacramento
Des Moines	Carson City	Santa Fe	Salt Lake City	Denver	Phoenix	Juneau
Topeka	Laramie	Anchorage	Houston	Las Vegas	Boulder	Pittsburgh
Oklahoma City	Detroit	Memphis	Louisville	Kokomo	Chicago	Twin Falls
Austin	St. Louis	Roswell	Birmingham	Spokane	Ogden	Oshkosh
St. Paul	Kansas City	Boston	Albany	Trenton	Harrisburg	Providence
Madison	Fairbanks	Annapolis	Hilo	Orlando	Dodge City	Concord
Little Rock	Newark	Augusta	Rock Hill	Raleigh	Columbus	Montpelier
Springfield	Atlantic City	Dover	Los Angeles	Columbia	Tampa	Butte
Indianapolis	Tulsa	Lincoln	Tucson	Nashville	Waterloo	Cleveland
Baton Rouge	New Orleans	Jefferson City	Idaho Falls	Richmond	Frankfort	Hartford
Montgomery	Tupelo	Jackson	Charlotte	Dayton	Palm Springs	Atlanta
Honolulu	Charleston	Lansing	Sioux City	Minneapolis	Miami	Tallahassee

Finish

Worldwide Scramble (page 165)

1. Italy; 2. Australia; 3. Hungary, 4. Canada; 5. Iceland; 6. China; 7. Turkey; 8. Brazil; 9. Germany; 10. Mexico

Number Crossword (pages 166–167)

9	9	9	■	7	5	■	3	7
6	7	8	4	■	3	4	1	■	5	0
8	6	■	1	5	3	■	9	8	1	2
■	■	4	0	5	■	3	9	0
2	9	1	7	■	7	3	8	■	1	8
5	0	3	■	2	3	0	■	1	4	0
3	1	■	1	1	1	■	3	2	5	0
■	6	0	3	■	9	1	9
1	1	6	7	■	3	5	3	■	3	8
9	6	■	9	2	1	■	9	7	0	1
9	0	■	2	3	■	3	3	3

Under Pressure (page 168)

It's over!

Answers

P Is for Preboarding (page 169)

1. packages; 2. pad (of paper); 3. paddle; 4. pages;
5. pail; 6. palm (plant); 7. panda; 8. pants;
9. parachute; 10. parachutist; 11. Paris; 12. parka;
13. passenger; 14. passport; 15. pasta; 16. paws;
17. pear; 18. Pegasus; 19. pelican; 20. pen;
21. pencil; 22. people; 23. Peru; 24. Phoenix;
25. photos; 26. pickle; 27. pictures; 28. pie; 29. pig;
30. pigtails; 31. pile; 32. pilot; 33. pineapple;
34. pizza; 35. plaid; 36. plane; 37. planet; 38. plant;
39. plaque; 40. plate; 41. "Please Ship" sticker;
42. plow; 43. pocketbook; 44. polka dots; 45. pony;
46. ponytail; 47. popcorn; 48. postal worker;
49. poster; 50. pot; 51. president; 52. propellers;
53. pull-toy; 54. pump; 55. purse
(other answers are possible)

Presidential Trivia (pages 170–171)

1. Jefferson; 2. Clinton; 3. Roosevelt; 4. Cleveland;
5. Lincoln; 6. Bush; 7. Ford; 8. Washington;
9. Kennedy; 10. Reagan
Answer: Eisenhower

Super Crossword (pages 172–173)

J	A	P	A	N		F	L	I	E	S
A	R	E	N	A		L	A	D	L	E
B	E	G	I	N		A	W	O	K	E
			A	S	K					
S	T	A	Y			H	E	L	P	M	E
T	E	L	E	V	I	S	I	O	N	S
S	E	A	S	O	N		T	R	O	T
			T	E	N					
O	Z	O	N	E		I	D	E	A	S
R	O	W	E	R		K	O	A	L	A
B	O	L	T	S		E	G	R	E	T

Spouting Off (page 175)

Carnival Rebus (page 176)

1. popcorn; 2. hot dog; 3. roller coaster; 4. Ferris wheel; 5. prizes; 6. cotton candy